Designing
Handmade
Rugs

Designing
Handmade
Rugs

Inspiration for Hooked, Punched, and Prodded Projects

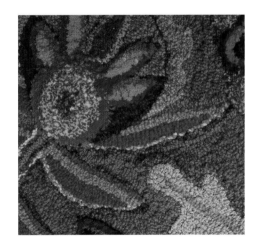

Annie Sherburne

STACKPOLE
BOOKS

To Netty and Liz
"Art is slow music – Let's Dance!"

Conceived, edited, and designed by Fil Rouge Press Ltd
110 Seddon House, Barbican, London EC2Y 8BX

Copyright © Fil Rouge Press Ltd, 2012

The right of Annie Sherburne to be identified as the author of this work has been asserted by her in accordance with the UK Copyright, Designs, and Patents Act 1988.

Published by
STACKPOLE BOOKS
5067 Ritter Road
Mechanicsburg, PA 17055
www.stackpolebooks.com

Printed in Singapore

10 9 8 7 6 5 4 3 2 1

First edition

ISBN 978-0-8117-1067-1

Cover design by Caroline Stover

FIL ROUGE PRESS
Publisher: Judith More
Editors: Jenny Latham, Nina Sharman
Designer: Maggie Aldred

Photography: Allan Titmuss
Additional photography: Lily More, Rosie Barnett, Gerard Brown

Contents

Where it started

I am a creative polymath; my hands, my mind, my soul, and my heart all think as they make. I try to make beautiful, useful things. I burst with feelings, with joy, and with faith, as I navigate and use my work to transform pain. My work comprises celebration, communication, expression, and catharsis. It is also a process, a journey, and a refinement. When I make, I receive contentment and an intimate understanding of how I am involved in The Creation.

My mom was artistic and musical, and the British television program Blue Peter made me believe that I could make anything. Also, I wanted things that I could not afford, so I filled my hours creating all sorts of things.

People liked what I was making, and at fourteen I had my first market stall selling sequin jewelry. I met Kaffe Fassett, who filled my mind with ideas of painting with wool. I sold colorful crochet and knitted items to London boutiques. At eighteen, I studied fashion at Central Saint Martins College of Art and Design, and then took an experimental textile course at Goldsmith's College, which destroyed my preconceptions and freed the creative process within me.

After college, I set up a business making textile-based jewelry (and visited India on the proceeds). I was discovered by renowned fashion designer Jean Muir, and went on to design and make jewelry, buttons, accessories, hats, and fabric for her for eighteen years. I pioneered patterned felt-making using industrial processes, and made patterned hats. However, when the 1987 economic crash destroyed the felt industry, I began to make tufted rugs, because I could work independently.

The late 1980s seemed apocalyptic: I felt powerless and desolate during the first Gulf War, with its burning oil wells. How could I, just one person, make a difference? I began to develop an ecological design practise, leading to my master's thesis: *The Ecological Thread*. I believe we can save the world.

Recycling—why?

Generally it is thought that we have problems in our world because of dwindling resources, but, in reality, we have created too much abundance. This abundance is tied up in products that have been designated as waste. For instance, if we throw our clothes away, or refuse to buy secondhand or used items, then this creates millions of tons of textile waste that go to landfills every year. This is unnecessary, because the true value in terms of energy and raw materials within those textiles has not been fully used.

The current global manufacturing system has, for decades, designed and created things for obsolescence, so that the demand for more keeps the factories profitable. The good news is that it is possible to transform this system with a long-term change in the manufacturing infrastructure. Factories and manufacturers need to "take back" their products and recycle them, but until they do, as far as textiles are concerned, there are plenty out there for us to make lovely rugs with!

If we create new lifestyles where we personally make many useful things, and only have what we love, or need, or what is eco friendly, around us, we might avoid facing an unnecessary scarcity of resources in the future. We face such scarcity because we have borrowed our abundance from the future. We need to get ten times more out of all our products than we currently do, just to reach a point where we can reverse what we have started. The Factor 10 Institute (www.factor10-institute.org) says that we need two and a half more planets just to carry on using new resources to make new products at the current rate.

So bearing in mind the above, we should start to use and recycle what we still have. We need to consider these strategies as being socially inclusive. The great thing about making rugs is that you can do them in a group, either working together on one rug, or making individual rugs with new friends in your local area. Making things in a group is educational, and great for bonding the generations, sharing knowledge, making friends, and dispelling loneliness. And with the advent of online galleries, such as Etsy, there is a place to show and sell your work and create a new economy.

Sketching the design for one of my fish rugs (see pages 10–11).

We can make gifts and do swaps too!

As the community strengthens and we become less manipulated by a decadent economy, we can envisage what we really need, and create a demand for a long-term vision for manufacturing that systematically values and recycles our raw materials. I am a fan of the argument in *Cradle to Cradle* by William McDonough and Michael Braungart, where production of materials, manufacturing, using the product, and then reusing the constituent materials link up into a perpetual circle, called a "closed loop." It shares and preserves nonrenewable resources.

Making is part of the gentle revolution where we stop handing over the job of decorating our homes to big stores. Market forces don't rule us, and we don't kowtow to profits, deadlines, and a means to an end. We don't want ends, we want new beginnings, a new rug, a new group to work with. Let's not consume our souls, let's stop consuming the planet, let's start enjoying it!

Cutting a remnant of colorful fabric into rag strips (above) and hooking them into a rug (right) at a cafe workshop event (see page 38). For advice on cutting and hooking, see the Getting Started chapter, pages 14-55.

Rites of passage

We are often left with clothes we cannot bear to part with when we, or our loved ones, make transitions in life. Children's clothes, special garments you wore when you were going out with your first love, even your wedding dress, or clothing that reminds you of those you have loved and lost—let's make rugs with them!

In dealing with possessions that people leave behind, we can extend, honor, heal, remember, and let go of our relationship with that person. Perhaps, most importantly, we can do something when we have no idea what to do. Making something new with what has been left behind gives us new ground to start again, particularly if we make a rug. It can be seen as creating a gift in honor of someone.

My own husband died nine months ago (from the time of writing), after a horrendous hurricane of destruction that ripped our family apart, caused by his brain cancer. He stopped fighting it, and he stopped fighting us and we were all reconciled. When he died, there was so much pain attached to the home where we had experienced his battle, that I gave most of our things away. However, there were some clothes that I could not part with—a beautiful checked shirt, some lightweight trousers, a T-shirt, and a very mangy old jacket. Wearing the jacket myself, which felt like I was being cuddled by Mark, I set to, cutting the shirt, trousers, and T-shirt into strips.

I made a fish rug.

For our family, this was a very poignant and healing thing to do. Before I was Mark's partner, and then wife, he had a store, where he put on an exhibition of my fish rugs. They were a series of rugs that developed after Chapman Root (American heir to the Root beer fortune, and whose family owns the design of the Coca-cola bottle) commissioned a number of fish rugs so that he could get out of bed and get to his bathroom without touching the floor. Subsequently, I made many fish rugs, which became so well known they made the front page of *The New York Times* magazine!

Mark told me that one had sold from the exhibition, and duly paid me. A year later, after he had sent me an enigmatic and hysterically funny Valentine's card, we were "going out together," as we say in England, and I went around to his place. The rug was proudly displayed in his own bathroom! Our marriage, friendship, children, and life together are now remembered and honored with a farewell fish rug made from his clothes.

I cut up the checked shirt and T-shirt while I wore the jacket. It felt like being cuddled.

"Mark's Fish" was made from his clothes, other
yarn, and bed sheets. This is an evocation of the
quickness of movement that is a fish. The shapes
come from free movement of my arm when
drawing, and an infill of sympathetic pattern.

Living with rugs

The White Horse Rug

This rug has become a symbol of my search for a more universally understood way of thinking about how to choose, work with, use, and reuse textiles in an environmentally friendly way. The simple shape of a running horse is based on white chalk carvings through grass that are found on various hills in the United Kingdom. The oldest horse, at Uffington, Oxfordshire, is 2,500 years old and has been kept going by repeated generations "scouring" or "recutting" the design.

Although most other chalk horses date from the nineteenth century, they all rely on the local community for their upkeep. Community is an essential part of sustainability—sharing resources, coordinating workloads fairly and efficiently, maintaining skills for the good of all, and protecting the chains of supply.

Displaying your rugs

The White Horse Rug can be placed on the floor, but because it includes white areas, it needs to be placed

My White Horse Rug reached the finals of the Classic Design Awards at the Victoria and Albert Museum, London, in 2006. It is made from my own brand of recycled rag yarn, factory ends, some naturally dyed yarn, and alpaca from British herds, spun by a water-wheel-powered mill.

where it will not get too much wear and tear. Hanging on the wall is a good alternative. I nail my rugs directly onto the wall, but you can use dowels if you wish. Sew a channel onto the lining to accommodate these, being careful not to impact on, or create indentation on, the face of the rug.

Making the White Horse Rug

I used 1 1/2 lb (680 g) white yarn and 18 lb (8 kg) green yarn to make this rug. For more information on estimating yarns see page 120.

Care and repair

Generally speaking, a new rag rug is springy and bright when you first place it on the floor. It then settles over a couple of months, and then pretty much stays at a slightly flattened, more integrated, and a little duller level for the rest of its life, perhaps getting frayed around the edges, and needing some TLC.

Some yarns are more robust than others. Place a delicate rug where there is less traffic, and it will last you a lifetime. But use your rugs. Move them to more lowly places as they get older. Make new ones for pride of place and as you redecorate your interiors.

Cleaning Traditionally, rugs are pegged onto a line and beaten. This dislodges the tiny particles of household dust that act like sandpaper, eating away at the base of each tuft and making a rug bald in patches. Rugs do not wear away from the surfaces, they wear from the base of the tufts. If you choose not to put secure your tufting with latex,

then the tufts of your rugs will be more vulnerable to pulling out, so beat with care and attention. Vacuuming is good. If you choose not to secure your tufting with latex, then be careful not to pull out lines of tufting!

I use a preparatory rug cleaning fluid on my rugs, and I dab by hand rather than using an upholstery vacuum, again so that the tufts are not pulled out in the cleaning process. I tend not to wash my rugs because the absorption of the water makes the rug too heavy and it never dries before it starts to smell bad. Unless it is a really hot summer, I do not recommend washing.

Repair Keep an eye on your rugs, and remember that "a stitch in time saves nine." You can patch areas that have completely worn away. I often add another backing cloth to my rugs, which I glue on with latex. This backing may have to be replaced. It does protect the rug, but many of the rag rugs that you will be making will not use latex at all.

Getting started

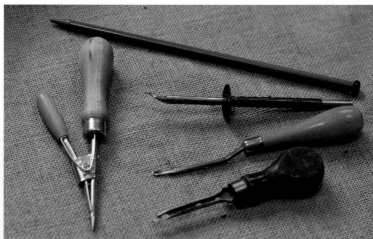

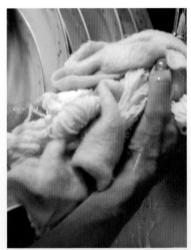
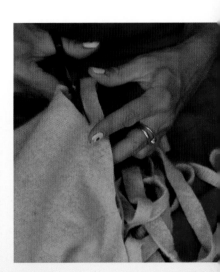

Yarns

Traditionally, rag rugs were made from scraps salvaged from worn-out clothes and domestic textiles. Today, we can still use these sources, and it's thrifty to reuse fabric from clothing that can no longer be used. You can also use pieces that still have some wear in them but may be out of fashion—it's up to you. You don't have to spend money; many crafters have closets full of materials bought on impulse or left over from previous projects, and rugs are an ideal way to put these stores or stashes to good use. If you don't have any on hand and need to buy some, then I would recommend you source eco-friendly yarns and fabrics that go the extra mile toward real sustainability and ethical trading practices.

Choosing yarns

For ease, I refer to each material that is used for the face (top) of the rug as "yarn," whether it is spun yarn, a woven fabric strip, or a piece of string. When you are deciding on the yarn to use for your design, first think of practical considerations: quality, strength, durability, safety (flammability), and flexibility (ease of working with the yarn). Then make your aesthetic choices: color, texture, thickness, cut or ripped edges, a single or multiple yarn palette. In respect of durability, do a break test, if you can pull it apart easily, it is not very durable!

Textile rags Worn or discarded garments and household linens, such as sheets and tablecloths, from your home or from a thrift store, are ideal for making rag yarn. For information on preparing salvaged fabrics see page 22. Wool, linen, cotton, and jute are all pretty durable, but do test them by pulling the rag and seeing if it breaks easily! Old fabrics and silks tend to be more fragile. Cotton and cotton T-shirts are great basics for rag rug making, and are hard wearing. Hemp, linen, and jute are really strong and I favor them if you

Rag strips cut from discarded cotton sheeting and dyed in vivid colors.

are buying new materials, particularly if they come from an ethical source.

Felted wool Felting knitted woolen textiles produces a firm yet soft fabric that doesn't fray or unravel and is extremely durable. For information on how to felt old woolen garments and prepare them for use see page 19.

Fiber If you can spin, try making an eclectic variegated yarn, using lots of different materials, such as fleece, video tape, feathers, raffia, lurex, sewing cottons, unraveled sweaters, netting from vegetable sacks, old pantyhose, pet hair, your own hair or hair from the hairdresser's, unraveled string, selvedge offcuts, sweepings from textile companies, odds and ends of braids and ribbons, in fact, anything! Wool fiber can be made into fine dreadlocks that will make fantastic loops and cut pile effects.

Fiber durability You can tuft directly with fiber (which is the unspun form before it is twisted and spun into an integrated yarn). The fiber form is not terribly strong, however, if used next to, or in combination with other yarn the use of fiber can be an aesthetic choice. Also, some rug makers, notably in Turkey, will tuft with fiber and then felt the rug itself when finished, so durability occurs then. It is a very interesting, exciting, and "rugged" technique that you may like to experiment with. Raffia is not terribly durable, but I have used it in major rugs because of the value of its texture. It is worth combining it with a stronger natural fiber such as hemp, so that over the years, as the raffia wears away, the hemp will remain and you will not have a big space in your rug.

String, rafia, and yarns spun from nettles or spun from recycled materials provide a delicious mix of textures.

Yarn, mixed fibers, and safety advice All yarns, synthetic and natural, are useable for rag rugs. Find odd balls of wool from thrift stores or use leftovers from knitting projects. Chunky yarns can be used singly, while thinner yarns can be twisted together. Knowing whether or not a yarn is synthetic is important for understanding flammability. If you want to sell your rugs, your customers need to know whether they are flammable. Wool is actually a natural fire retardant, and is used in airplane upholstery for this reason. Many synthetic fibers melt. Also, if you place a rug made from synthetic fibers by an open fire, it is at risk from embers. Wool is the queen of fibers because it is strong. Silk is strong too, but it is expensive. Look for sustainable sources. Silk can be very fine; if it is, then use it for cut piles, for fine work (as in the shell handbag project on page 98), and for dyeing, because it takes color well and has a beautiful luster. Fragile fine fibers and yarns can be mixed with strong yarns. Although finer yarns may wear away over time, this results in an aesthetically pleasing patina that will add to the life cycle of your rug (just like an old, well-loved and worn teddy bear). Linen, hemp, jute, even string, can be great additions to the color palette, and, more particularly, texture. They are all strong and are hardwearing when they are looped. Some of the rougher-textured yarns in this group shed fibers when made into cut pile, because the fibers don't adhere to each other in the way that wool does. Wool has barbs on it; most bast fibers don't. This is why they don't felt unless mixed with wool fiber, which actually will felt around them. Having said this, they do make great paper, because they melt into each other, releasing starches that stick the fibers together. Another yarn worth experimenting with in this group is actually paper. Bear in mind that there is a constant dialogue between aesthetic and practical. Do wear tests and don't expect something of great beauty but limited strength to last well as a hall carpet. It's horses for courses!

Flotsam and jetsam There's lots of mileage in materials that are usually thrown away: fine fruit netting, bits of sea-weathered fishing net from your beach vacation, unraveled plastic cement sacks, old cassette tape. Even though you can use plastic bags, it's not a good idea. They are very flammable and today's bags are made of biodegradable cellulose which will disintegrate, so your work will fall apart in time. Many bits of flotsam and jetsam would be best added to some home spinning.

Ribbon, cord, and string Using ribbon is really effective, but it is expensive. Cord, braid, and string all create fantastic effects and textures. When cut, some cords have cores of white or colored cotton—it can be really exciting experimenting with anything you can tuft with. Again, always do strength and flammability tests.

Eco materials

Textiles are either renewable or non-renewable. Renewable textiles come from natural sources that are biodegradable. Non-renewable textiles are mainly made from oil and don't biodegrade, but can be used again and again. Even if the materials you use aren't eco-friendly as regards their source or production, they still need to be reused, rather than going into a landfill.

Environmentally friendly design currently involves a great deal of recycling and reuse. For the designer, it can be more of a challenge because there are inherent aesthetics within recycled materials. In the 20th century, designers and customers became used to specifying and choosing, so designers tended to work with virgin materials. Finding a source of raw materials and yarns that are recyclable, and even more beautiful and inspirational than 'virgin' materials is, therefore, a way to go straight to eco-heaven. Hand-spinning flotsam and jetsam with fleece, and then felting it, makes glorious, strong yarn to work with, in terms of color, variation, texture, and environmental integrity.

Here are some eco-friendly choices if you are buying yarn for your project:

Shoddy and mungo In 1850, Benjamin Law used the new spinning machines of the industrial revolution to recycle rags (shoddy) and the fiber that fell from the mechanical spinning process (mungo). The resulting fabric was used until the 1960s, often dyed navy to overcome the irregular colors of the raw materials. The famous "Crombie" overcoat favored by London's city workers was made from this recycled fabric. However, with the advent of marketing "pure new wool" in the 1960s, customers began to demand "new" fabrics, so they threw these garments away. The demand for recycled cloth and the industry of making it all but disappeared.

The 1980s saw the beginning of the textile environmental movement, and the importance of a financially viable recycling industry became a vision. A grant from the London mayor's office helped me to retrace the production chain, and make 2 metric tons of shoddy yarn. My yarn has now been used by many ethical fashion designers, including Ada Zaniton. The yarns on page 20 are examples of my shoddy and mungo yarn dyed with natural dyes.

Organic wool This is produced from organic livestock, which in itself is a step toward better animal husbandry.

Organic cotton Though better than ordinary cotton, it is problematic because of its excessive use of potable water and displacement of food production so, in the long run other natural fibers, such as bamboo, may be greener choices.

Organic color-grown cotton Invented by Sally Fox, the olive to brown to cream color range has been bred into the fiber itself, avoiding the need for chemical dyes.

How to felt

Mistakenly, you may have shrunk your best wool or cashmere sweater beyond redemption, so you already know how to felt a garment. However, in order to be in charge of the process, the quickest method is to wash a wool or cashmere garment on the hot cycle of a washing machine, and then dry it in a tumble drier at a very hot temperature. The more ecological way is to wet it with hot, soapy water, roll it in a towel and rigorously roll the bundle back and forth in much the same way as when making felt from wool fiber. Cut the resulting shrunken garment into strips and you have wonderful, non-fraying, soft material for rag rug making.

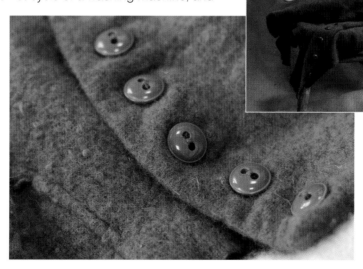

Organic hemp String-like, hemp is strong, takes dye well, and is one of the most sustainable fibers because it takes little from the environment. It replenishes soil, and binds soil on marginal lands with its strong root network, thus reversing erosion.

Rare breed yarn This has many different qualities, textures, and colors. Buying and using this yarn supports an important industry that preserves diversity in breeds by making the rare flocks economically viable.

Hand-spun yarn There are many specialist hand-spun yarns available online. Rachel Matthews kindly shows us some of her yarns and how to spin with a drop spindle opposite. Buying hand-spun yarn enables you to work with unique materials and supports small businesses. In addition, we can develop new markets and begin to reverse economic gloom if we buy from each other.

Recycled yarn made from industrial waste

A good source of ethical, eco-friendly yarn comes from women's co-operatives, which gather fiber and yarn waste from industrial enterprises and spin this into

My own "Eco-Annie" yarn recycled from discarded knitwear, and spun following the old production routes that created shoddy yarn (see page 19). These yarns are carded with a 50 percent pure new wool mix to give strength and "handle." Hand-dyed with natural dyes, the skeins are variegated indigo and cochineal. The yellow is a weld dye on organic yarn from Wensleydale sheep.

yarn. Sari silk from India and Nepal are good sources, and there are Indonesian enterprises that were set up after the 2004 Tsunami. There is also an unexpected source of high-quality fiber from the soya food-processing industry. This yarn is luxurious in feel and is currently used to make silken carpets. I hope that entrepreneurial companies might appropriate this yarn for the home crafting market.

Paper yarn Made from twisted rag papers, this is surprisingly robust. It is worth considering as an additional textural quality.

Industrial waste yarns spun by women displaced by the Indonesian tsunami. The waste warp threads are plied with a single color to give partial coherence to what would otherwise be consistently random production.

Spinning yarn

Rachel Matthews of the wonderful London shop *Prick Your Finger* uses a drop spindle to make her own yarns for knitting, weaving, and rug making. She spins fiber around existing recycled yarns and can add other elements as she goes along. This technique gives you the potential for controlling color and texture within your designs, and for breaking away from the norm to make really unique and original rugs. After spinning, the yarns can be felted. These yarns have been used in the café rug on page 41, and again in the textured

pillow on page 55. This is a case where recycling adds aesthetic value to your rug making because of the unique quality of the yarn.

Rachel adds netting from fruit packaging, old video tapes, stockings, frayed nylon rope—in fact, all manner of found fibers and threads. I recommend that you take a course in spinning to really maximize the creative potential of this method, but for your information, I have given a very brief three-step synopsis of the process of drop spinning below.

1 Rachel pulls the carded fiber out, ready to spin.

2 Here she connects the fiber to pre-loaded yarn on the drop spindle.

3 While the spindle is spinning, Rachel draws out the fiber.

Hand-spun yarns by Rachael Matthews and business partner Louise Harries of *"Prick Your Finger."*

Preparatory techniques

Cutting rag strips

Cutting the strips for a rug can take a long time, but there are short cuts that do not detract from the quality of your work. Some makers advise you to use a craft knife, and to measure the width of the rag strip exactly, but I don't do this, partly because the flexibility of textiles makes it difficult to make an exact cut. Fabric stretches with the application of pressure from a knife blade. I think that using a good pair of sharp scissors and your own good judgement to "cut by eye" is fine.

T-shirts can be cut in a continuous strip by going round and round. Cutting a woven fabric on the bias means that the edges don't fray, but the rag strip itself will be stretchy. Cutting woven fabric along the line of the weave gives you a good strong strip; sometimes it frays a little, but this can add to the texture of the rug, and is not necessarily a bad thing.

The ideal width depends on the thickness of the fabric itself. Loop up a bit of the cut fabric and see how easily you can pull it through the backing fabric using a rug tool. The width is dependent on how easy it is to make stitches, and on the aesthetic choices you make. For instance, a thick blanket that was used in some of the projects was about 3/8 inch (1 cm) wide.

Cutting rag strips can be a meditative process once you get going, and you will soon have a large pile of rag ready to use. Alternatively, cut and rip for speed and efficiency! However, doing this does create some fiber dust so you might want to wear a mask. Ripping the fabric also causes fraying, which does create extra texture when you tuft your rug. When you have prepared the rag strips, you can wind them into a ball, or if you are planning to dye them, make some skeins. See page 25 for skein preparation instructions.

Cutting strips from a felted cashmere sweater.

Transferring your design using a grid

Now take your paper design and make a scaled grid. Then transfer the design to your backing fabric.

Lay your backing fabric flat on a table or on the floor. Place some newspaper under the fabric so that you don't end up drawing on the table or floor too! Many of the projects in this book do not require the fabric to be stretched, although you can also stretch your fabric onto a vertical frame.

Using a pencil and ruler, draw a scaled grid over the original drawing (see diagram opposite). Then scale up the grid to the finished size of the rug (for sizes and ratios, see box below). Using a fine permanent marker pen and a ruler or a long straight edge, draw the scaled-up grid onto your backing fabric. If you have a ruler, great, but if not, any long, straight object will do—a baton of wood, cardboard, or packaging. You will need a tape measure to measure your grid, and a set square, which can be a large book, or any other accurately squared domestic object!

Copy the design carefully into the scaled up squares on your backing fabric using a permanent marker.

Sketch of the design for the White Horse Rug (see pages 11), with the grid drawn over it in pencil, ready for transferring onto the backing fabric.

Using grids to transfer designs

You need the grid to reflect the simplicity or complexity of the design you are scaling up. If the design is complex, smaller squares will make copying the design "by eye" easier. The white horse is a relatively simple design to transfer. If your finished rug is 3 ft x 6 ft (1m x 2m), then I would recommend scaling-up to a ratio of 4 to 1, but for a more complicated design I would recommend 6 to 1 or even 8 to 1. The joy of using grids is that you copy from a small original design only what you see in each square. You refer all the idiosyncrasies of those lines to the shape of the enlarged square drawn onto the backing fabric. It's brilliant because it's easier to copy an abstract shape relative to a corner or a distance along an edge than keep the whole design in mind at once. Try it—it's very satisfying to do!

Working on a frame

A lot of my work is done on a large vertical frame, but a Brown's tool (see page 30) is not easy to use on stretched fabric, so other "punching or pushing" tools should be used on stretched backing fabrics. Usually your hands need to access both sides of the frame easily, so I would recommend using a lap-sized frame—when your work is larger than the frame, be prepared to move the frame from area to area.

In order to stretch the fabric onto the frame, place a length of fabric over the frame and knock a nail into the center of one side of the frame. Stretch the fabric across and secure it with a nail in the center on the opposite side. Now stretch the fabric along the top edge and place a nail into the center of that edge. Do the same along the bottom edge. I draw freehand onto the fabric using a black felt pen, while referring to my sketches. I work directly, and make shapes that I feel look right, rather than making an accurate scaled guide from my original drawings.

Dyeing

Color is the most important tool of design, and making color through dyeing is an art, craft, and skill in itself. As an eco designer, I would like to advise you on best practice, because some dyes not only are toxic to produce, but can pollute if toxic residues are washed down the drain.

• If you use chemical dyes, always fully exhaust the dye bath. This can mean using less dye to start with, over-dyeing the same yarn to achieve density of color, and then using other virgin yarn to soak up the remaining dye for paler shades.

• Direct chemical dyes can be used in a microwave; this technique enables most of the dye to enter the fiber; therefore, there is minimal harmful waste.

• To achieve bright colors many crafters use Kool-Aid, which contains non-toxic (edible) coloring.

• Natural dyeing is really enjoyable, but the colors are entirely different from those achieved with chemical

Kitchen cupboard dyes

Your kitchen contains many foods that can be used as dyes. Master dyer Debbie Bamford told me that good dyes were too expensive for most people, but in medieval times, everyone loved and wore bright clothes. They used hedgerow dyes, but these would fade very quickly. So always do color- and light-fast tests. Salt helps to make a dye fast.

A selection of natural dye stuffs, clockwise starting from the left: fustic, natural dyes in powder form, weld, logwood chips (from sustainable sources).

Clockwise starting from the left: red onions, Spanish onions, red wine, coffee, beetroot, teabags, salt, and turmeric.

The following ingredients are pretty fast:
Golden onion skins: tan
Red onion: greeny beige
Red wine: stains gray
Turmeric: wonderful bright yellow
Tea and coffee: shades of brown and tan
Henna: shades of orange
Paprika: yellow

The following ingredients are pretty, but will not last for long:
Beetroot, red cabbage, raspberries, blackberries, and soft fruit: pinks and lilacs

dyes, often as a result of ten different chemical reactions occurring during the process. You need to do color-fast and light-fast tests, because it would be a pity to spend hours making a rug that fades. You can use indigo, madder, and weld as your main spectrum, just like the ancient rug makers. However, indigo is ecologically problematic as it requires deoxygenation of the water to achieve the beautiful blue. Ancient "eco" methods are disgusting, including the use of fermented boy's urine! I tried, but could not last the distance! Big star to those who succeed! I recommend the expertise of master dyers Jenny Dean and Dominique Cardon, as found in their book *Natural Dyes*.

Natural dyes require mordanting, which enables the color to "bite" into the fiber, and sets the dye. The mordants are often heavy metals. Eco natural dyers simply do not use these. Currently people still use alum.

Preparing the yarn for dyeing

A skein is the best form for dyeing any yarn, because it presents as much of the surface of the yarn as possible to the dye. Skeins should be quite loose so that the dye can circulate and penetrate, but with enough ties so that they keep their form and do not tangle. All yarns and rags can be dyed in skein form. Wet the skeins with a little liquid detergent; squeeze out any excess liquid, and then place in a heated dye bath with room to stir.

1 Make a big loop of yarn and secure with a loose knot so that it's easy to undo when dyed and dried.

2 Add lots of yarn to the loop by turning between your hands. Keep an even tension.

3 Leave a long cut end, and make a number of loose but firm single looped knots around your skein to keep the yarn from tangling.

Dyeing the fabric

Muslin, silk, cotton, and wool work well with natural dyes and the lighter the fabric is in color, the better. White or pastel colors work the best. It's helpful to use a large old pot as your dye vessel. If you want to avoid stained hands, wear household gloves to handle the fabric that has been dyed. The step-by-step sequence here shows how to dye fabric (I used old wool blankets) with stripes of color. After each color stripe stage the rest of the dye bath didn't go to waste—I used it to dye some strips of cotton sheeting in solid colors.

Once dyed, cutting the striped fabric into a continuous strip gives a variegated rag yarn. The fabric can also be used in the textured pillow project to make variegated leaves (see page 52).

YOU WILL NEED

- *Natural dye (either powdered or in organic form)*
- *Two old pots (or as many as the dyes you want to use) for the dye baths, preferably stainless steel, but any pot will do*
- *Hot water*
- *Suitable fabric or yarn*
- *Soap*
- *Wooden stick or dowel longer than the width of the dye bath*
- *Wooden spoon*
- *Household latex gloves*

1 If you are using powdered dye (tumeric here) mix it into a paste with some hot water, and put it into the dye bath. Otherwise, boil and strain your organic matter and put it into the dye bath.

2 Add enough boiling water so that the dye bath is just under halfway full.

3 Prepare your fabric by washing it in clean, soapy water. Here, I am using a skein of yarn and part of a woolen blanket.

4 Squeeze out all excess moisture. You can blot it further by squeezing the fabric in a dry towel. The purpose of wetting the fabric is to enable easy, even absorption of the dye, but if it is very wet, it will dilute the dye, add bulk and displace too much liquid from the dye bath, and, most importantly, wick color too far. You only want to dye part of the fabric and yarn.

5 Fold the fabric and yarn over the stick. Balance the stick on top of the dye bath, and allow the fabrics to sink into the bath. Allow to simmer for a few minutes, depending on the strength of the dye. If the dye is weak, you might leave to simmer for longer.

6 Lift the fabric and yarn out of the dye bath to check for desired color intensity. Place a bowl under the fabrics to catch drips, then take them to the sink to rinse. Squeeze out excess dye under cool running water, and try to not allow contamination at this point to the other areas of fabric and yarn.

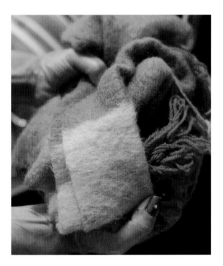

7 Place the extra rag strips in the dye bath and simmer for a few minutes. With a bowl underneath to catch drips, lift the bundle of rag strips out of the dye bath and squeeze out excess dye under cool running water. Set aside to dry.

8 With a different dye, make up another dye bath. Next, fold dyed fabric and yarn over the stick, and balance the stick on top of the bath, allowing undyed ends to sink into the new color. Repeat step 6.

9 The striped fabric and yarn have a range of subtle earth colors. The 'natural' stripes make little flecks like stars when you tuft with it. Alternatively, arrange the fabric on the baton so that the dyes run into each other, creating subtle color gradation.

Tools and techniques

Hooking and punching tools

Over the years I have collected old and second-hand tools. There is social history to be found in this, as well as a few tabletop contraptions that promise to speed up the process of rag rug making. However, the hand tools are my favorite, mainly because I like to move around with my work and I like to "get in there!" I studied embroidery, and although this was a radical, fine art-based college course, I do like to do fine work too. Many of the hand tools illustrated here produce the same technique in different scales. You can therefore use a rugged yarn or a fine yarn, make a thick rug or make a fine velvet. They are versatile and don't restrict you to a mechanical device.

Rug-making hooks

There are many variations of tools, but only really two basic processes. Punching is about "pushing" the yarn through a backing cloth. Hooking is about "pulling" the yarn through a backing cloth. (There are also many names for these processes.) The more sophisticated punching tools involve threading the yarn through an "eye" in the tool. There is a stopping device that dictates the distance the yarn can be pushed through. You catch the yarn on the opposite side and adjust the loop length. These tools are generally used on a stretched frame, working from the back. However, you can use them on a loose backing cloth and push through from the back if you wish.

Brown's tool This is my preferred tool; it has a lever function to grab yarn and safely pull it through backing fabric. (Illustrated on pages 30–31.)

Thick knitting needle This is used to make holes where necessary in the backing fabric—for example, when pulling a cut shape through, as in the textured pillow project on page 54. You can use it as a basic punch needle too, although a more blunt peg, thick pencil, or whittled twig performs this function better, because the needle is smooth and slips too easily.

Clockwise from the left: Brown's tool, thick knitting needle, punch needle with eye and adjustable pile height stopper, punch needle with eye, hole maker for punching, latch hook.

Rug punch needle with adjustable pile height disc and eye Some punch needles have discs to adjust the pile height. This is useful. You thread the yarn through the eye, plunge it through the fabric, and the disc stops the pile length as you withdraw the tool to plunge again into the next tuft. In practice, catching the yarn with your free hand on the other side of the fabric is necessary.

Punch needle with eye This tool is used in the same way as the punch needle above, except that the pile height is only accomplished by catching the yarn after it has been plunged through the fabric using the tool. The eye catches the yarn. The thickness of yarn is limited by the size of the eye. There are fine punch needles that can be used for fine velvet work, but I have invented a new technique to use in combination with these punch needles to make contemporary velvets (see page 98).

Hole maker This tool is used for making holes, but it also has a spiral thread, which has friction. It could therefore, to some degree, also be used for punching.

With many of these tools their historic development and use may well have evolved to meet specific and sophisticated techniques employed by our rug making forebears. My theory is that if it works for you, use it! Develop your own techniques, and share these with your fellow rug makers too.

A pile maker This is used to make cut lengths of yarn for latch hook techniques (see page 33).

Latch hook This allows you to work with pre-cut lengths of yarn and to make knots, like in Rya rugs, which come from Finland. The knot is similar to a ghiordes knot, which is used in traditional Persian rug making. Using a very loose backing cloth is preferable.

Ye Susan Burr

Described as a hooked rug machine, Ye Susan Burr is an old-fashioned wood and brass tool designed to speed up the process of making punched rugs on a frame. I found one for sale on auction website eBay along with all its original documentation. This one dates to 1951, but the illustration looks like the machine originally dates back to the 1920s. This tool emulates the action of my own mechanical machine, and probably would have speeded up the process in adept hands.

The Brown's tool

Introducing the Brown's tool

When I work by hand, I favor the Brown's tool. I also have a hand-held machine that I use for my commercial rugs—which has been known to break down at inopportune moments. There is a fabulous shop in Chiswick, London, called EcoAge, which is the brainchild of eco-warrior, stylist, and ecologist Livia Firth (the wife of Colin Firth). Here, beautiful design is achieved by using only eco-friendly and ethically sourced products. I was commissioned to make rugs for EcoAge, but my machine broke. I tried every vintage tool I had, and found that the Brown's tool was fast, accurate, and equivalent to the quality of my machine. I fulfilled my order on time and saved my important commission. I commend it to you!

Using the Brown's tool

The elements of the tool:
• A pointed tip;
• A latch that opens on a spring;
• Two handles are connected to the spring; when they are squeezed, they open the latch, and when released, they close the latch.
The tool pokes through the fabric, you squeeze the handles, the latch opens to grab the yarn. You release the handles, the latch closes around the yarn and you pull it through to create loops on either side of the stitch of backing fabric.
It is particularly good because:
• You can use many thicknesses of yarn and rag.
• You can also work without a frame, which means it's easier to work on your lap, and easy to transport around.
• It is easy to pick up, so everyone can use it. Children and complete craft novices contributing to communal projects can be seen using Brown's tools.

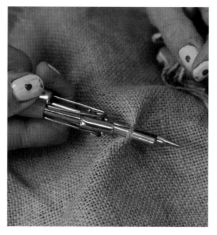

1 Push the pointed edge of the tool through the backing cloth, picking up two or three warp and weft threads.

2 Make sure that the latch is pushed past the fabric stitch that you have made, and then press the two wooden handles together to open the jaw.

3 Place the yarn between the open jaws and allow the sprung lever to close. Pull the yarn through.

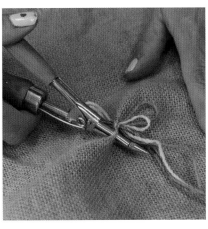

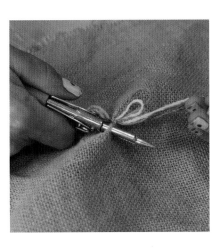

4 Now the end of the yarn is on one side of the stitch and there is a loop on the other side. You need to evolve a personal technique where your tufting is even; however, you can adjust the loop heights manually.

5 Again, push the pointed end under two or three warp threads of your backing cloth a few threads to the side of your first stitch. This creates a line of fabric between two lines of tufts.

6 Make two looped stitches every time you pull yarn through. Imagine that each stitch loop is 1 inch (2 cm) in circumference, then place in the free yarn where you grab with your tool's jaw. You are making two tufts for each stitch.
I recommend experimenting. It makes more sense when you are doing it!

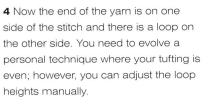

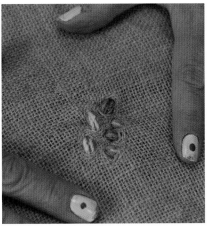

7 See the beginning of a line of tufts here. Subsequent parallel lines of tufting push the tufts up vertically. If you wish to make a single line for the purposes of your design, the tool should tuft at a 180-degree angle to previous stitches.

8 This is how two rows look on the back. When you make a row next to your first row, the tufts will stand up. The next row should be about four warp/weft threads away from the first. Make sure that your tufting is not too tight.

9 To make a cut pile, cut through the loops with a pair of scissors. If you know you want a cut pile, make your tufts a bit longer, cut through the loops, and then trim back neatly.

Hooking techniques

Working with rags

The technique for working with rags is similar to working with yarn. If the rags are quite thick, they need to be "jiggled" gently through the backing cloth.

Rags are pulled through as single strips. They can be left looped, or cut. If you look at the pillow project (page 54), you'll see that quite a lot of the rags have been cut. The surface texture is really interesting because the cut ends pack together like little stripes or 'dashes.' The tufts of rags are bolder than yarn tufts, so that, in design terms, the scale of mark making is strong. This goes really well in interior design because furniture is big, and floors are big too, so having a

textile that compliments this larger scale gives you a lot of mileage in terms of X-factor impact. Most store-bought pillows, curtains or drapes and rugs have fine surfaces, and rely on their outside edge to define a visual impact (of squares, oblongs, folded drapes). The surfaces of textural rag rugs read well at a distance too, and I find this a very exciting extra dimension for interior design.

The looped ends of rags are very strong, and springy. I have the pillow in my home, and everyone makes a beeline for it, to touch it and to relax into it. It is a really good example of applied art; it really animates my living room couch!

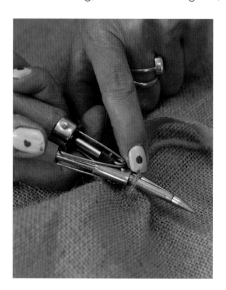

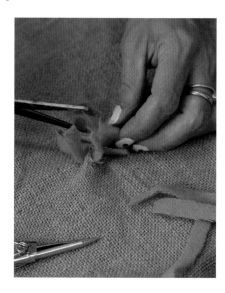

1 Push the tool through the fabric as far as the base of the jaws, picking up two warp/weft threads. Open the jaws and place a rag strip in the tool. Close the jaws and start to pull the rag strip through the backing fabric.

2 Pull the rag through until you have a loop, as shown. Release the jaws and move on to create the next loop, two to three warp/weft threads from the first loop.

3 If you want to create a pile, cut through the loops and trim them to the height required.

Latchhooking

The latch hook is a tool used for Rya rugs. It is used with wide-hole canvas. Ready-cut lengths of yarn are doubled up. The hook stitches through the canvas, and then pulls the loop of the yarn through. The loop stays on the hook. Next, the hook is pushed forward to catch the two tail ends of yarn and pulls the tail ends through the loop. You then have a little slip knot that you pull tight to make a single, neat, secure tuft.

1 Pushing the latch hook through the fabric.

2 This picture demonstrates how the little latch closes when you pull the loop of yarn back through the canvas. It is a pleasurably simple and clever device.

Using a pile maker

The pile maker can be as simple as a piece of cardboard, but shown here is a wood block with a lengthways groove cut into it, so that it is easy to pass one blade of a pair of scissors along to cut the yarn.

1 Winding yarn evenly around the pile maker.

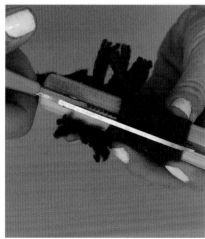

2 Cutting the yarn: the bottom scissor blade fits into the groove.

Punching techniques

Two vintage punch needles are illustrated in this section. One has an adjustable "stop" to maintain pile height, and the other "simple" punch needle relies on you to adjust the pile height manually. Essentially what happens is that you use the tool to push yarn through stretched fabric. You need to be able to access both sides easily with both hands. However, this doesn't mean that you are limited to a small-sized rug, because you can move your backing fabric onto a frame as you finish one section.

1 The punch needle is a hollow tube with a disc to stop the tool at the same distance every time you push it through the fabric. To thread the needle, make a loop with the yarn.

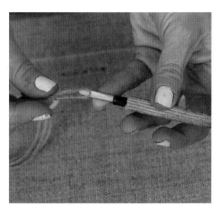

2 I use a thin crochet hook pushed through the needle from the sharp end to catch the yarn and pull it through to thread it into the tool.

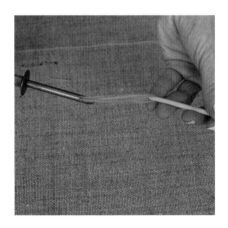

3 There is an eyehole on this needle. Threading the yarn through this eyehole secures the yarn for pushing it through the stretched backing fabric.

4 Allow the yarn to pull through loosely, and position the needle ready to push through the backing fabric.

5 Push the tool through the backing cloth with one hand.

6 Be ready to catch the loop that is made on the other side, so that when you withdraw the needle to make the next stitch, the yarn loop stays in place.

7 It is very satisfying to make a row of stitches. Space the stitches a few warp threads apart.

8 The loops should be neat and of an even length. You can leave them as loops, or cut them for a cut pile finish.

Simple punch needle

The simple needle has an eyehole to attach the yarn and hold it in place as you plunge the pointed end through the fabric. You can work from either side of the fabric, using a sense of touch to measure the distance between stitches on the underside, or simply by turning the frame backward and forward as you work.

1 Push the needle through the backing fabric. You can make a neat line of stitches as you go.

2 Catch the yarn to make a loop on the other side of the backing fabric. Your hand makes the stitch height, so you may wish to turn the frame regularly, or work from the back through to the front, so that you can keep a neat and regular pile height.

Other tools and materials

Sharp scissors are the most important tool after the rug tool itself. They cut the fabric and are essential when working on the rug. You then use them to cut and refine the surface of the pile, and to trim ends when finishing. Any sharp scissors will suffice, but when cutting strips, a long blade is expedient in terms of time and effort. Working on the rug, you are more likely to need smaller hand scissors.

A flat edge to draw straight lines when making grids.

Set square or other means, such as the corner of a book, for drawing a 90-degree angle and straight lines.

Frames and hoops If you want to use the punch needles in a traditional manner or indeed do any fine work (other than my new invented method for making velvet in the purse project), then you will need to stretch your backing cloth onto a frame. You can make samples using an embroidery hoop. If you are using a frame, then you can use a staple gun or nails. Align the direction of the grain of your fabric with the square of your frame. Put one nail or staple in the center of one of the sides. Pull the fabric at a right angle to this and put the next nail in center of the opposite side under tension. Continue working your way around the frame in this manner until the fabric is tight like a drum skin.

Backing fabric The base cloth for rugmaking has traditionally been feed sacks, or hessian. I use a professional cloth made from very strong manmade fiber and woven at $4^{1}/4$ yards (4 meters) wide. This is not necessary for domestic projects. All these fabrics have a loose weave, and are relatively strong.

Edging tape If you look at the backs of rugs in stores, they have usually been finished with a rough cloth and edged with woven binding. This is your choice. If you choose to back your rug, you can stick or sew a tape around the edge. The edge is the place where most wear occurs. You will not need to back your rug so often if you use a tape. I don't use tape because it adds too much extra bulk to the edges of my rugs and presents a tripping hazard. Turning the corners makes this area even more bulky. Also, the rugs only need backing every four years or so unless they are in areas of high traffic. See opposite for the way I edge rugs.

Rubber solution glue and brush Use a small household paintbrush and a rubber or latex solution painted onto the reverse of the rug for durability; see opposite.

From left to right: backing fabrics, edging tape, brush to apply glue, and rubber glue solution.

Backing techniques

Traditionally, rag rugs did not have a glue backing. When you make a rug, you will probably enjoy the soft flexibility when you roll it, but to prevent any of your hard work being accidentally pulled out and to make the rug more durable you can paint rubber or latex solution glue onto the back.

1 Trim excess backing cloth, leaving a margin of 1 inch (3 cm) to fold under and thereby create a neat edge.

2 Lay the trimmed rug onto hessian backing, and cut another piece the same size as your rug, again with a margin of 1 inch (3 cm) to turn under and create a neat edge.

3 Paint the rug back with latex solution glue. Do NOT allow it to dry because you will now stick the hessian backing onto the latexed rug.

4 Gently separate the edges and fold them in to meet each other—this is important because it defines a good clear edge to the rug.

5 Where the rug and backing fabric are shaped (e.g. scallop and heart rugs) and the edge is " going in" you need to snip the edges to create "ease." Here, cut into the sharp dimple in the top of the heart no further than the edge of the rag stitches.

6 Start to stitch the edges together. You can do a simple binding stitch, or a blanket stitch if you prefer. Keep going until you have completed the sewing and the rug looks neat and tidy on both the back and the front.

Beginner's workshop

Marking out the ogee stripe pattern using a black marker pen on the base fabric.

In London, there is a groundswell of communal making. Knitters arrange to meet on underground trains to make sweaters and chat. On some nights, sewing takes over the whole of the restaurant "Leon" in Spitalfields market. There's a revolution of vibrant Women's Institute groups too (I am a Shoreditch sister) full of skill sharing, practical activism, and community. It is the urban family in action. It is delicious! There are sewing bees and quilt-making groups, meeting regularly, enjoying friendship, food, wine, and tea, week by week, and making intimate, meaningful things for each other's homes. I wanted to teach the skills to make rag rugs. We have so many odds and ends of clothes around and it's really easy to do.

Organizing a beginner's workshop

I contacted a boutique/café called Eat, Shop, Do (where you can do all of the above things). They already hosted workshops and we arranged to teach rug making for free. In the late summer, I packed some bags with interesting textured yarns in a harmonious color palette, a large piece of backing cloth, and a box of Brown's tools and scissors. Through online groups I tweeted, facebooked, and e-mailed everyone I could think of who liked to make things. We were joined by curious visitors and tourists, and watched by some of the other visitors to the café.

The design

For four hours, we worked on a simple rug design of "stripes with subversion." I drew

straight lines, and then broke out into an "ogee" pattern where the stripes transformed into leaf-shaped pools of color. "Ogee" is one of the first formal structures to learn and play around with in traditional textile design; it is made of mirrored "s" shapes that curve together and away from each other again and again. As a design structure it's like an armature. I kept it simple, but you can embellish, subvert, and refer to this simple structure of a stripe and an ogee that is always in "repeat," making it easy to take into fabric and wallpaper printing. William Morris used a basic ogee for many of his famous designs.

The workshop

There were spaces for at least twelve people along each side of the table. I showed each person how

to use the tool. They chose the yarn they liked, and started to tuft a straight line immediately in front of where they were sitting. The lines began to meet up. Participants left and more people took their places. They tufted lines above and below the lines and even made starts on the leaf shapes and color pools.

Finishing the rug

I finished the rug afterward, and cut strips from a beautiful but threadbare green wool blanket to make large areas of plain background color. This was an important aspect of the success of the design. The eye likes to move around and see conversations between pattern, color, and form. These areas of pale green are a restful foil for the dancing colors and textures in the stripes and patterned leaf shapes. Because people were given free rein in choosing colors, the rug could have been chaotic, but this simple single color device strikes a balance.

Designing your project according to limitations

To be a designer, I believe there are two core attributes. The first is personal: simply to know that you want to be a designer. Until you know, your energies can be dissipated. The second is situational: to design within the specific limitations that are present at that time. This could be few materials, little time, or a small room. It might sound odd, but this will give you the greatest possible freedom

because you push your boundaries within a defined form.

When I look at Persian carpets, I can tell when a yarn or color has run out because there is a change or patch in the pattern. There is also a tradition in Japanese ceramics of making a deliberate mistake that acknowledges that beauty resides in imperfection. My own great teacher, Kaffe Fassett, taught me about color by how he orchestrates changes. It is the creative X-factor that lifts a work, it's often intuitive, and often an economic necessity.

If we take these principles into a group, where many individuals chose to come together to work with limitations, with fragments, remains, and offcuts, I wonder what new creativity will happen, and what new art will be made.

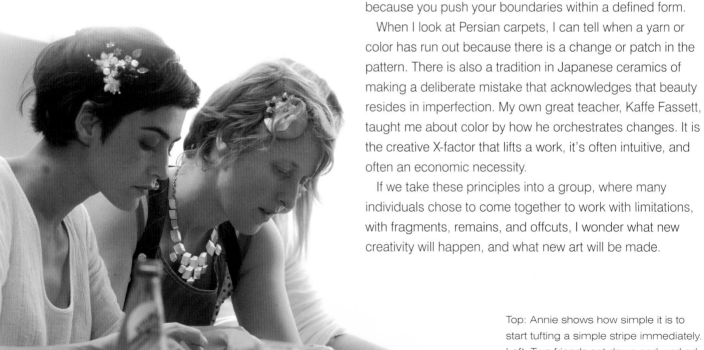

Top: Annie shows how simple it is to start tufting a simple stripe immediately. Left: Two friends sat down and worked side by side.

The finished beginner's workshop rug.

Beginner's workshop rug yarns

This was made from a large selection of harmonizing yarns and rags. The green area was made from a woolen blanket. It constitutes just under half of the rug and you will need approximately 5 lb (2.27 kg) of yarn for this section. For the yellow edging you will need about 4 oz (113 g) of yarn, but you can prepare more, because this yarn can also be used in the mixed area. The pink key in the pattern on page 121 represents a massive mixture of yarns and rags. On the straight edge, the yarns are worked in stripes. On the wave side the rug is worked in an ogee pattern where there are defining outlines of parallel, mirroring leaf shapes. The leaves are infilled with blocks of different colors to create the design. Please study the pattern on page 121 and the photograph above. I recommend that you provide 12–15 lb (5.44–6.80 kg) of mixed colors, yarns, textures, and rags for this part of the rug.

Color palettes

Where to start with color? It is visceral, interpretive, emotional, definitive, descriptive, and disruptive. Color is visual music, evocative, tasty like food, scented, and full of memories. Because this is a book on design I don't want to be prescriptive on your use of color. I'd like you to notice which colors you love and feel confident working with. Combinations of color are like personalities. Color takes shape in objects and in light, with shadow, form, and texture. Colors mix lightly in pointillism, drone deeply if physically mixed, or vibrate on edges when next to each other. They converse, argue, clash, soothe, recede, and crash into you.

For this book's purposes, let's say that colors are definitive vehicles for the pattern and form of the materials we are working with. Like the sensual interfaces of our imaginations, they seduce us into enjoying the repetitive labor of love that is making a rug.

How I work with color and why

I have to work in a mess. I can't make my work unless balls of yarn and fabric and general detritus of living surround me. This is because those materials are inanimate. They don't think or move as fast as my creative mind. If I tidy up, then I'm not making, I'm ordering. Johannes Itten, the great Bauhaus color theorist, says that there are two ways to work with color, one where you just know and do, and the other where you work to formulas. Choose the method that is right for you.

I look around me at the yarns and see a combination that sings to me. I choose my palettes in this way. In the journey rug (see page 68), I pushed my own personal color language to the edge, evoking memories of 1950s interiors, 1960s oranges and purples, 1970s pop culture clashes, spurious new ageism in the 1990s, sleeping beyond fear of the dark, making new planets, lying on a stony beach, and English 20th-century art and tensions.

To get to this point, I worked with single evocations. This is how I would recommend you choose your color palettes. However, try not to use intellectual equivalents. Don't say this blue stands for the sea, or this red stands for the dress I wore on a particular day. Find the actual shade, the brilliance or darkness, the exact combination that you actually saw in front of you, and use that. In tasting your cooking you wouldn't say the red onion stands for a red apple, or the vinegar stands for blackcurrant coulis. And when smelling you wouldn't say that a lavender toilet cleaner stands for your designer scent. Look at the actual colors and see how they make you feel.

A simple technique to create a palette is to start with the rainbow, and exclude one color, for example, red or yellow. This creates harmonious tension. Contaminate

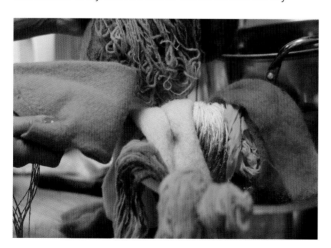

Left An acid-green synthetic dye creates a visual "pop" against a selection of natural dye colors (left).

the colors you have chosen; make them darker by adding black, or lighter by adding white. Or add red to each. Play with ideas. Keep some uncontaminated, add black to some and white to others. Mix the colors with each other. Another technique is to use equivalents. For blue, only use gray; for red, use pink, for green, use turquoise; for yellow, use tan; for orange, use brown; and for purple, use deep indigo. I am describing something I do when presented with lots of colors, where it is actually a very sensual choice, like trying to select from a chocolate box. Essentially, the equivalent colors will have elements of high color, light, dark, and depth.

A different technique is to create two groups of similar colors, and tie them together in random "balls." Make a design that relies on only two colors, and then execute that design using the two mixed balls you have made.

Cut-out silhouettes like those in the hare rug (see page 94) might work—I learnt this technique by studying the knitwear of Kaffe Fassett. The sensual and slightly random order of color changes means that within a simple pattern endless slight variations and unexpected meetings occur between shades. The whole has coherence, but shimmers with life. In a rug the tufted, colored loops can mix optically on the face of the rug. You can mix four strands of black and red yarn in many variations—for example, one black and three red, or two of each, or three black and one red.

When I undertake a commission, I ask for color samples from, and photographs of, the room where the rug is going to be placed. I match colors to these samples. I have accumulated a vast selection of yarns: factory ends, and yarns that conform to other criteria, such as recycled, rare breed, from sustainable sources, and eco fibers. The resulting harmony is always extraordinary; the rug just slips into place as the colors all sing to each other.

I will sometimes choose the darkest or the lightest colors in an interior and play with contrasts. The other way to work is like a painter, where you choose colors because you want to work with their promised dynamic. Sometimes you can be presented with a disparate group. Then it is good to put colors into different groups that do work together. I often talk about the nature of two elements, and of dialogue. If you divide colors into two groups, they might work well in two different parts of a design. It might be that there is one disruptive color in there that needs to be taken out to make the rest harmonize. Basically, just play with it till you have your happy balance.

Left: Hot colors—pulsing pinks and orange and red—with a good tonal contrast, so plenty of opportunity for pattern. Pale pink and turquoise are foils to set the flames alight.

Right: Bright, light, dark, mixed, and pure color. Choose two colors, make them dance, then add two more, make motifs, and let them swim around on a background.

Creating color samples

Part of the inspiration for the design process is mixing your yarns to create interesting harmonies of color and texture. Making bunches of yarns and fabrics is like an artist mixing paints, and will give you quick and often enjoyably unexpected results—at the same time, you are creating a color palette to work with in your new rug design.

The top of the tufts you make will indicate what the yarns will look like when they form the rug surface. You don't have to cut the loops every time, because the cut pile is often darker and richer than the loop. You can use them both (cut loops and loops) in the same rug for subtler differences. Experiment by using fine yarns, first single colors, then combinations. Then use rag strips, uneven handspun yarns, in fact, anything you have chosen. Then mix them together. You are mixing not only color, which will have a pointillist effect, but also texture.

1 Wind your chosen yarn selection around your fingers.

2 Cut the ends of the looped yarn. You can also do another sample where you don't cut the yarn.

3 Tie the bundle tightly.

4 Look at the tuft ends; this is what your mix will look like in the rug.

5 Examples of different tuft samples—see how the white lace splays out, how the denim rag is stiff, and how the purple and gold organza is ethereal.

Colors and stripes

On my first day in the textile department at art college I was given the task of creating a striped design. Was this a boring first day? Possibly, for students full of ideas and ambition, but so-called simple stripes are a real challenge, because the possibilities for variation are infinite.

How many colors will you use? How wide are the stripes? Will the width of the stripes vary? How will you balance the tonal differences of the colors? Stripes go in one direction in a multi-dimensional world. They have an ability to create order, yet still express pattern and decoration. Once you have designed a good stripe, you can place it next to any pattern, and by linking color, tame the pattern without letting it lose its vibrancy. Why? How? Because in simple visual conversation, the eye likes to move and compare. Busy decoration can be simplified by the eye into a single element when compared with another well-balanced, simple element. A single color field next to pattern allows the eye to rest. Pattern against pattern requires energetic engagement, while pattern against stripes is dynamic and vibrant without being too overpowering. For example, consider how the startling cerise pink stripes of Bedouin dresses sit next to the fine embroidered chest panels.

Stripes on their own are stunning. Artists who use stripes brilliantly include Mark Rothko, Sean Scully, perhaps even Brigit Riley. In the Victoria and Albert Museum in London there are amazing examples of brocades from the 17th century where the proportions of fine and wider stripes, subsequently put into mirrored repeats, are delicious. The craftspeople and designers who worked with these fine silk weaves expressed the finest subtleties of their abilities and made the most extraordinary textiles; their virtuosity

I consider stripes to be parallel lines—once you have got a good stripe you can bend it into a motif or form.

included fine graduations of colors within each stripe. We can achieve this by mixing yarns optically. I like to use four threads for my rugs. Using two colors and rows, I start with four red, then three red and one blue, then two red and two blue, then one red and three blue, and finish with a row of four blue threads to create a similar effect. This mixing can also create a three-dimensional effect, when the eye reads the color graduations as shadow.

The use of a stripe in a rug can be marvelous. A stripe is so unyieldingly, irrefutably directional. It will slim a room, direct a flow of footsteps along a hallway, lead you to a door, take you up stairs, and if you use the stripes horizontally, they will announce a landing, widen a space, create a border, or act as a foil to another pattern.

My favorite vintage stripes, counterclockwise from near right:19th-century French theater, Galliano's degree collection, my mother's 1940s scarf, Berber headdress, Bedouin dress.

Advanced stripes

This is where you can subvert the idea of a stripe. Stripes can be considered to be parallel lines. Stripes are the jumping-off point for creativity. They can define, radiate, change direction, move away from each other, and come together again. They can get thicker and thinner. Japanese pebble gardens use stripes to radiate around points. A pebble thrown into the water, wave patterns against the beach, striped cloth that is folded, upholstered or draped around a form. Personally, I like to think of Paul Klee, who "took a line for a walk," when I break out from the line and double or treble it for visual emphasis (see my sketch on page 46).

I also use a formal, accurate wave stripe as one of my infill patterns in my own rugs. When I do this, I am breaking up an abstract area. I also use this same wave to carry a pattern across borders between

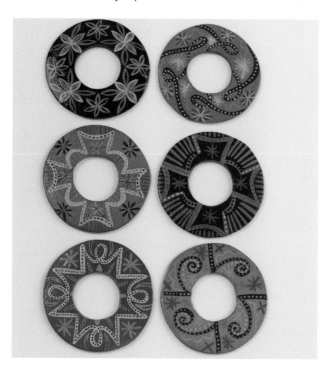

shapes. This creates a dynamic surface visually, but also enables me to use the principles of pointillism where the eye mixes colors that are placed closer together in a subtly shimmering vibrancy that flat blocks of color don't have.

Another subversion of the stripe is to use color and or texture to change the line itself. Native Australian tribes paint lines and put white dots along them. The line becomes so vibrant it seems to transcend the surface on which it has been painted. Another way to create dynamic along the line is to change the colors at intervals, perhaps by graduating color changes.

The choice of color is a separate issue. Consideration needs to be given to the tonal value of the color in relation to the colors around, as well as to the overall color scheme. It is worth looking at the ikat work of artists such as Mary Restieux and Ptolemy Mann to see how color graduation can be used to great effect.

The subverted stripe has five other attributes to play with, namely the pile height, the texture, and the variation of width of the actual stripe itself. The stripe can also be "split" to create islands within it, in which there can be other colors, textures, and patterns. The stripe itself could even be a block of pattern, texture, or other more complex form that then gets used as a single tool within a larger striped pattern. (Imagine here the equivalent of brocade ribbons, used as stripes in their own right.)

In many ways, these insights into the seemingly simple stripe are in fact definitive ways of using the "line" within contemporary rug making, and can be applied to all your design choices and decisions.

My hand-painted jewelry: spots animate the lines.
This is inspired by native Australian artwork.

A selection of designs showing how to animate
simple lines, used in my rug designs.

Texture

Texture is apprehended not only visually, but also through touch. In many of my rugs, when you sit on them, you will find soft areas of alpaca that contrast with scratchy hemp, and velvety cut pile next to the tough, springy feel of loop pile wool.

One more tip is to experiment with the length of the little tufts. In the white horse rug (see page 12), the grass is long and can have textural hemp in with soft wool, so it feels and looks like grass. A long-pile floppy yarn can look wonderful against a shorter pile too. Again, you can make a pattern or definition on the surface of a subtle rug design just by varying how much you make different surfaces.

I was once asked to make some completely white rugs for an exhibition, which was a strange request to make of an artist known for her color work! I made massive landscapes in white, using every type of white and cream yarn I could find, and varied the surfaces to good effect.

The same yarn selection as those used in "Natural Land-scape" in a different abstract design. "The Rag Bower," displayed below, was made by sewing strips of rag, line by line, onto both sides of a recycled chiffon scarf. Opposite are examples of materials with vastly differing textural and tactile qualities.

"Natural Landscape" made entirely from eco yarns, accumulated for sale in my store and use in my own work, and contextualized within my environmental textile research for my master's degree.

Making leaves

YOU WILL NEED

- *Scissors*
- *Felted wool fabric*
- *A punch needle (or knitting needle) for making holes if necessary*
- *Brown's tool*
- *Backing cloth*

Contemporary rag rug techniques mean pushing the boundaries and being experimental. Since I work with fabric, it is interesting to see how far it is possible to manipulate the raw materials within the limitations of the technique. Sewing things onto the backing fabric and tufting around them is a possibility, but I also like working to the extremes of the craft process itself. I think there is a lot more mileage in cutting shapes with slits, and looping them through the backing cloth to make large, defined tufts. In the flower pillow on pages 54–55, I have manipulated these shapes to make flower motifs, but I am already wondering if I can develop an integrated fabric by tufting on both sides, and whether the tensions will distort the backing fabric into interesting forms.

1 Cut a teardrop shape from your felted wool fabric, and cut a small slit in the round end.

3 Push the pointed edge of the leaf through the slit in the base of the leaf.

4 Gently tighten the pointed end against the rounded end to create a knot.

2 With the Brown's tool pointing inward on the edge of an imagined circle (1½ inch (4 cm) in diameter approximately), insert it into the backing cloth and grab the thinner end of the teardrop shape and pull it through. Use a punch or knitting needle to enlarge the hole for the Brown's tool if need be.

5 Manipulate both parts of the ensuing knot backward in order to create the double effect. The Brown's tool should be moved 60 degrees around the circumference of the imagined circle to make the next leaf. You will fill the circle with other tufting to make the stamens of your flower.

Making flowers

1 Cut out the petal shape. I used the fabric from the dip dyeing project, making use of the stripe.

2 Fold the oval petal in half and cut a small slit in the middle, lengthwise.

3 Hook one end of the petal shape through your backing fabric.

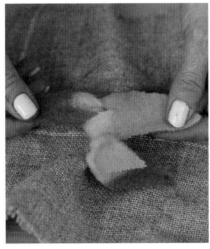

4 Pull the two ends of the petal flat on either side of the stitch in the backing cloth.

5 Pull one pointed end of the petal through the central slit where it appears on the other side of the stitch you've made in the backing cloth.

6 Manipulate the double petals to lie against each other.

Flower pillow

I am so excited about this pillow—or cushion, as we call it in England! It is very springy, the colors are great in bright sunlight, and making it was totally joyful. I invented it as I went along, playing with texture, using favorite pieces of yarn as if they were jewels that I was setting in a precious ring.

I made pompoms and used the leaf and flower techniques from pages 52–3 to make the pillow's three-dimensional appearance. I used rags, sheets, old netting, hemp, ribbon, stockings, and sheets, and the main impetus was "contrast." The pillow feels as different texturally as it looks.

I backed the pillow with part of a blanket, and put a good pad inside. I can't wait to make some more!

YOU WILL NEED

- *2 lb (907 g) of blanket (cut into strips and dyed)*
- *2–3 oz (56–84 g) assorted threads (for the pompoms)*
- *Brown's tool or equivalent tool*
- *Pillow pad measuring 26 x 22 in (66 x 56 cm)*
- *Hessian base cloth, measuring 28 x 24 in (71 x 61 cm)*
- *Backing fabric measuring 28 x 24 in (71 x 61 cm)*
- *Latex*
- *Needle and thread*
- *Scissors*
- *Pattern on page 121*

Pompoms

If you don't know how to make pompoms, and in case you are nowhere near a computer, basically, cut out two circles about the dimension of your intended pompom from card stock. Cut out a circle from the middle of each, and wind yarn from the center around the outside and back through the center until you have covered all the cardboard, and the hole in the middle is almost full.

Then slip scissors between the tightly bound wool on the outside, and between the two circles of cardboard. Cut all the way around. Pull the cardboard circles apart enough to

tie yarn tightly around the center. Pull off the cardboard circles (they might tear, but that's okay). Then trim your pompom until it is round! Use the ties to sew directly onto your pillow project and tuft around it.

Building a design

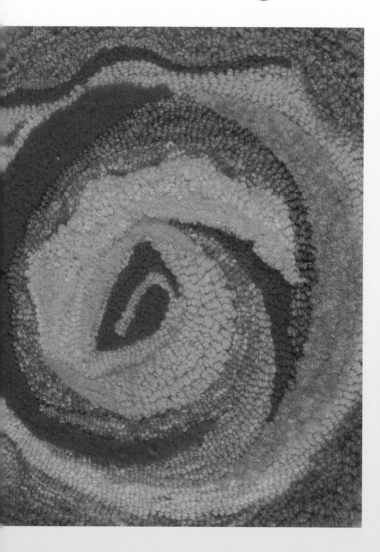

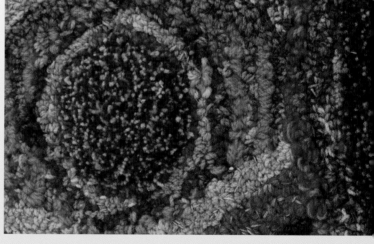

Simple shapes

The foundation of modern art and architecture is the Bauhaus—the famous German school that combined crafts with fine arts. From my personal encounter with Bauhaus I gained a confidence in simplicity and a self-evident foundation for working with materials, processes, images, and colors that is nothing less than creative logic. Johannes Itten, Walter Gropius, and Wassily Kandinsky established a basic foundation of irreducible simplicity, of square, circle, and triangle and the three primary colors. These elements exist in space, and can be seen as primary forms underlying all forms. The objective of Bauhaus was to enable the creation of unified works of art, design, and architecture, using glass, clay, wood, metal, textile, and stone, and to free the mind from all preconceptions to enable creativity.

A parallel example is found in the music of minimalist composer Lola Perrin, who can hold an audience spellbound in recitals of exquisitely crafted pieces based around a single note on a piano, middle C. With a secure base, in music, art, architecture, and eco-design, every elaboration and development becomes possible.

Today there are many more materials and processes to which we can apply the same understanding and integrity by using the same foundations of pared-down simplicity. In environmental design we are now developing processes that are sympathetic with cycles in nature. Some of these ideas draw from research known as biomimicry, where truth to materials and processes mean we can use materials appropriately, with natural reuse and recycling built in.

I always go back to basics to refresh, refocus, and concentrate once more, like a seed, ready to grow into something new.

Some of the simple shapes I draw to help build a design. I start with a circle or a square, keep my pencil on the paper, and move it almost as if the line is a dancer. Making a line is like watching a thought-movement.

Circles rug

The idea behind this rug is a flower growing. It developed from a commission; I was asked to interpret a naïve gypsy carpet that came from a bohemian apartment in Paris, which was featured in a French interiors magazine. On the original there were gaudy roses on top of a black background. The image was so evocative; it was dreamlike and reminded me of the smell of the Guerlain perfume *L'Heure Bleu*.

In this rug the circles represent the petals of a flower (possibly a rose). The flower uncurls from the compact center. In roses, like layers of fine tissue paper, the innermost petals are slightly disheveled, folded, and twisted. Then a concertina edge escapes, and blossoms into a new petal. Fragile petals uncurl from the center, plumping out and becoming voluptuous. And soon I am lost into creating imagined shapes circling outward—a ripple against a smooth moon-shaped edge, then a double ripple with an inner moon edge, and an outer ripple, in raspberry, saffron, blood, and lilac. Suddenly, at the edge of the rug, my design reverses into a shadow memory of emanation, with rippling echoes of maroon pretending to be black.

The rug is made by choosing color combinations that, in turn, make islands of shapes. The height of the pile (whether looped or not) and the sculpting of the cut pile areas are key features of this rug. It is actually lovely to sit on, because there are so many textures to touch. The high areas of pile are springy and the cut pile is soft.

YOU WILL NEED

- *5–7 lb (2–3 kg) yarn*
- *Brown's tool or equivalent tool*
- *Two pieces of hessian base cloth, measuring 3ft x 3 ft 1 x 1 m), plus turnings (see page 120)*
- *Latex*
- *Needle and thread*
- *Scissors*
- *Pattern on page 121*

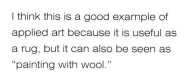

I think this is a good example of applied art because it is useful as a rug, but it can also be seen as "painting with wool."

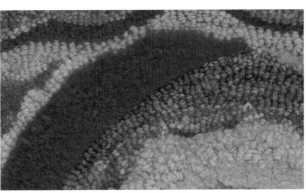

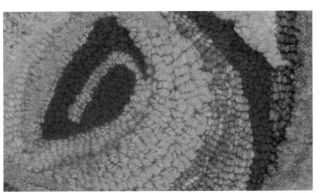

Symmetry

Many traditional Persian rugs appear to have double symmetry—a border, maybe a roundel in the middle. In a Garden of Eden rug (see page 84), paradise rugs, or prayer rugs, there is single symmetry. Symmetry is so familiar that it is very reassuring to see. There is a sense of order, even in the most elaborate designs.

It is a really enjoyable way of building pattern and design. I start by mirroring a motif around an imagined central line. By turning the design 90 degrees and creating another central line, I can mirror the motif a second time.

I make what I call "mod-trad" rugs, where I loosely draw a structure on my backing cloth, consisting of

Thumbnail sketches show how various motifs will look in "mod-trad" form. It is a very rich and satisfying form of pattern making; it almost makes itself, which is an enjoyable process, because there is a sense of watching it unfold.

a border and central and diagonal lines, to create a linear foundation. Then I hand-draw motifs in a loose mirroring manner. This makes the rug look handmade. I see no point in attempting to emulate the perfection that exists in hand-knotted Persian rugs, or the boring repetitive accuracy of the machine made rug. However, I do like to play with the familiar, recognizable traditional design form.

I am inspired by the Bloomsbury Group and the Omega Workshops. They decorated every surface, and made textiles, needlepoints, prints, drapes, and rugs that played with domestic design forms, inspired by Impressionism, Fauvism, Constructivism, and Modernism. They are romantically definitive of an innocent, domestic aesthetic. I love William Blake, dramatic sunrises at winter solstice, the warmth of tweed, slippers, a fire, and a hearthrug. My symmetrical rugs are made to be part of visions such as these.

Symmetry rugs

The rugs on these two pages all make use of symmetry. The rug shown top near right is what I call a Mod-Trad rug (see page 62), inspired by ideas of boats, rivers, and aboriginal points marking journeys (see page 48). This rug also shows a subverted double symmetry because the colors change, but the pattern structure remains symmetrical. The Mod-Trad rug that is shown bottom near right is inspired by the imaginary painted ceilings of heavenly gypsy caravans.

Top far right is a rug entitled Red Violin—there is a joyous imaginary Parisian café, where artists paint and musicians meet to play red violins while lovers dance. The rug shown bottom far right was my very first Mod-Trad rug. A border of oak leaves from Albion, shells from the birth of Venus, and compasses made of flowers surrounds the window to a rainbow sky of creation. There are many lotus pads watching and waiting.

Above: Two examples of Mod-Trad rugs.

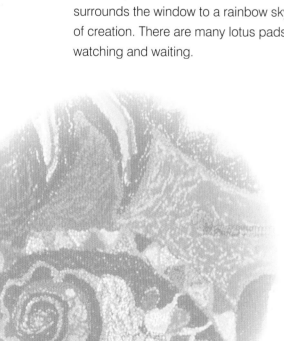

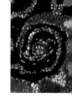

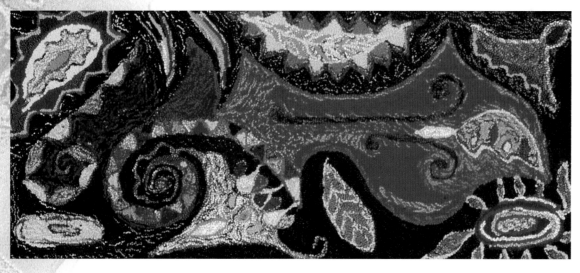

Above: Red
violin rug.

Right: My first
Mod-Trad rug.

Geometrics

The inspiration provided by geometrics is probably one of the most fruitful sources that any artist can work from. Geometry is structure. In the real world, geometry makes the forms that we inhabit, but it is also the basis of pattern. It is marvelous to play with. Starting with children's building blocks, there are patterns that we intuitively make. Then there is the great art form of Islamic architecture, where palaces and temples grow from a simple circle drawn using a string line and one fixed point. All subsequent information is gathered by measuring distances from single points on the original circle. This technique is also found in medieval wood carving and in celtic art.

Sources of geometry that inspire me are De Sjtil and the Bauhaus. This arguably is the foundation of modern art schooling, where form was stripped back to the basics—cone, cube, tube, sphere—for drawing, designing, and making the forms that have defined the modernist art movements of the twentieth century. I love the work of the English modernists, Barbara Hepworth, Paul Nash, and Ben Nicholson, where color is often displaced by a love affair with shapes. I also love the beadwork and painted houses of the Ndebele people. It's the women who are the artists. I admire their attitude—they get an idea and they just do it, which means that their houses are bright and joyful jewels in the African landscape. Their superb beadwork is also like wearing portable art.

My journey rugs are very influenced by all the sources mentioned above. Like the Arabic architect, I start with one point, one line, and one division of a space. I do use lengths of yarn alongside a ruler, because I like to make my patterns and shapes by using my eye rather than formal measurements. Whether you use formal measurement or not is really up to you. When

In this sketchbook I am playing around with arrangements of geometric shapes as rug designs. The bottom left-hand corner shows sketches from traditional design sources at a museum or library.

I was at college, artists who decided on structures and methods first were called systems artists. It could be counting, like in the Fibonacci sequence or other mathematical sequences, it could be working with a grid, or any other methodical inspiration.

This is a contemporary rug in the traditional Berber house of Douar Samra, in the Atlas mountains of Morocco.

The journey rug

I want to talk about a series of rugs that I have been developing over many years. They are called journey rugs. I am inspired by words and ideas as well as by visual shapes, colors and textures. In fact, a smell or a sound can also help me to visualize a design.

The rugs are linear. Imagine standing, looking down around your feet, then taking one step forward, then another, then another. This might be the length of a hallway in your house. How nice to think of those four steps as a journey! Our homes are special to us; they represent safety, they reflect us, they are our inner sanctums. We can have a journey along our own hallway, and make an otherwise nondescript part of our home into something very special.

Look again at those four steps, and begin to see the "landscape" of those steps change. I start at one end, one corner, and begin to sketch a few shapes, and I imagine I am floating over the four steps. They don't have to be rigid; they can flow into each other.

I use geometry, in that I have a ruler; sometimes I measure accurately, and sometimes by eye. In Persian geometry, buildings develop from

YOU WILL NEED
- *Approximate quantities of key colors*
- *8 oz (225 g) beige*
- *3 oz (85 g) cerise*
- *2 oz (56 g) purple and green*
- *2–3 oz (56–85 g) dark green and dark turquoise*
- *1–2 oz (28–56 g) purple*
- *2–3 oz (56–85 g) dark green and black*
- *1lb (453 g) reds and oranges*
- *2 oz (56 g) turquoise*
- *5– 6 oz (142–170 g) orange*
- *small amount black, orange, yellow, and blue*
- *2–3 oz (56–85 g) each of cream and pale pink*
- *5–6 oz (142–170 g) purple and red*
- *6–8 oz (170–225 g) Sherwood green*
- *1–2 oz (28–56 g) green and 3–4 oz (85–113 g) pale pink*
- *Brown's tool or equivalent tool*
- *Two pieces of hessian base cloth, 18 in x 5 ft (45 cm x 1.5 m), plus turnings (see page 120)*
- *Latex, scissors, and needle and thread*
- *Pattern on page 122*

circles drawn on the ground from one fixed point. Measurements are then made from the circumference, and more points are created on the circle. I define the shape of the rug, and work with a ruler to divide the internal space. I use freehand, kitchen bowls, and plates. I sketch lines and get a feel for the new rug. I work in books, doing thumbnail sketches, and I use these when I go to the backing cloth as well.

I like to work within what many people would consider a chaos of color and materials. You don't have to, but it can be very liberating to try this method, because you can look around you and see color combinations you would not have thought of otherwise, and then you just pick those materials up and work directly with them! No dyeing, no trying to match colors! In this way I can respond immediately to the inspiration of the moment, maybe a bit like writing a song, or doing interpretive dance, or following thought reveries.

I have various marks that I like to make, including infill and stripes of varying proportions. A striped wave is fun, graduating from one color to another by changing the proportions of the colors when I mix the threads together. I mix a dark color with a light color, which creates a speckle, and I combine a high pile, a cut pile, a low pile, different textures of yarn, sometimes using a sparkly yarn (although sparkly yarn isn't usually strong enough for walking on).

There is so much to consider when making a rug, but it can be very, very simple, or quite complex. The important thing is that you enjoy the process. You are not in competition. Let your work speak back to you, because you are on a journey of creative discovery.

  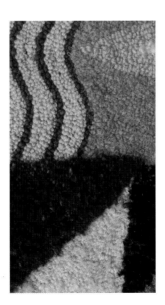 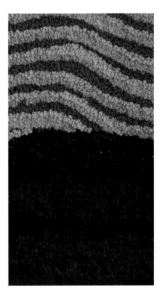

In creating this rug I evoked many memories: interiors from the 1950s; orange and purple from the 1960s; clashing pop culture from the 1970s; and spurious New Ageism in the 1990s, to recall but a few.

Borders

Borders are one of the greatest tools for completing an artwork or a rug design, as well as an excuse for decorative embellishment, because they deal with something that is not only obtuse and difficult in the real world but also impossible conceptually, namely "the edge." Minimalism and modernism reject anything extraneous such as borders, leaving only edges, which are seen as beautiful in their own right. In contemporary design practice, you have the ability to say "no" very firmly to borders, or to go totally wild and use them as and when you wish. In fact, we can now use the ironic border, the witty border, the incongruous border, and make rugs for minimalist interiors, because they look fabulous with all that space around them.

I am talking about the rug as art. At college, I was taught by a great conceptual artist called Ferris Newton. We quickly dismissed the idea of a frame as an acceptable part of a painting. Think about how silly it is that a generic object must be attached to the edge of every work of art just to define its function to be considered as "Art." We spent hours discussing the edge of textiles, the concepts of totality and integrity within a piece. Of being brave enough not to have a frame on the edge to announce the value and context of a piece of work. Ferris, notably, made his own paintbrushes as works of art in themselves, to be hung on the wall on a nail that he himself had forged.

Almost arbitrarily eternal rolls of textiles are produced, which are made to be cut up and made into something else that will "complete" them—a dress, a pillow, a curtain or drape, upholstery, and even, in the case of the environmental artist Christo, a wrapping for the Riechstag building in Berlin, or curtains for the Grand Canyon.

But we are lucky! Rugs are those unusual textile objects that are satisfyingly complete in themselves. They are usable paintings; they are applied art. You are free to do what you want with them. They can have a border if you want—they don't have to though!

Borders can be very elaborate; they can be virtually all there is. They can be used like baseboards or ceiling moldings, to define a large, empty space.

Advanced shapes

If you do want a border, then it is likely to be part of the edge of the rug. So start with the shape of the edge. It can be a line in itself, the line that relates to the floor that the rug is placed on, or the line that relates to the walls or the furniture in the space that you have made the rug for. It can even have a shape that relates to an idea. My fish rugs (see page 10) developed after I had made jewelry for the great British fashion designer Jean Muir CBE. Her simple and exquisitely cut clothes had room for what she called "wit." My jewelry was shaped and painted, and created a "dynamic" impact on her simple, timeless clothes. After many years playing around with the effect that different shapes had as jewelry or "portable works of art," I started making shaped rugs that create a similar sense of dynamic movement in interiors. At the time, open-plan loft living was all the rage. Such a large space doesn't need to have a square or oblong rug, but can have a different-shaped rug that is used to enhance a "flow" from one space to another.

So a border relates to an edge. It is an interface between one area or place and another—you can have borders within rugs too. In my range of "mod-trad" rugs (see page 62-5), I play with the traditional form of rug making where borders are used on edges, but also to frame or edge internal areas. I make a simple pattern within my borders. The pattern can be formal, repetitive, or symmetrical, but sometimes I subvert a simple repeating form like a wave or zigzag and add lots of colors, usually within the limited color palette that was originally chosen. This is a very economic and ecological way to work, because I can use up the smallest fabric scraps, and I have lots of really different shades in my store of odds and ends. This way of working is difficult to copy in manufacturing

When I draw like this I pretend that my hand is dancing. I like to challenge myself to make unexpected shapes—these are two pieces of my hand-painted jewelry.

systems, and it sets apart the craftsmanship that can be achieved in handmade contemporary rug making to a high aesthetic level.

First published in 1856, *The Grammar of Ornament* by Owen Jones is a great design resource. Also think about architecture. It has many decorative borders; there are the Greek key symbols, and the crenellations of castles, and friezes, to name but a few. Take inspiration from stripes, ribbons, and brocades—they are all effective. The edges of Kashmir shawls from the Victorian era are elaborate. There is the whole history of borders of the sari—in fact, of so many "ethnic" costumes. The edges of the skirts and textiles of the hill tribes between China and Vietnam currently fascinate me. The workmanship is breathtaking. The tribes make their costumes painstakingly, and then dress like exquisite birds for parties, with layers of pattern where borders are essential within the layering process.

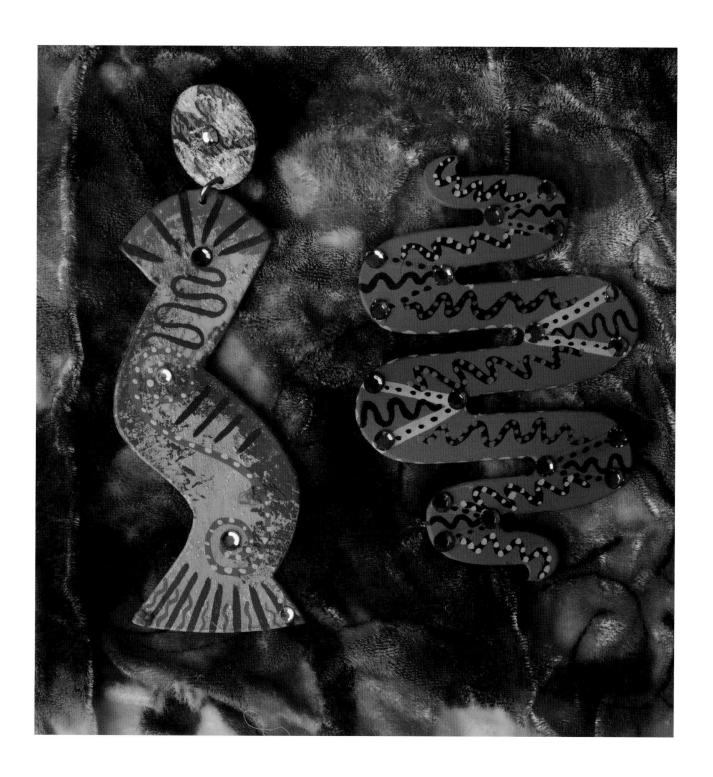

Scallop-edged rug

Traditional rag rugs sometimes incorporate a scalloped edge. In the 1980s, many artist and designer rugs featured scallops. They were in vogue in interior design at the time.

Contemporary rag rugs do not have to follow or imitate, but can reinvent, reinterpret, and subvert the designs that went before, as well as drawing from other contemporary design inspiration sources.

What we are dealing with is the edge of a rug, which does not have to be straight. Other rugs in this book are shaped. This project subverts the edge in a different way. It follows a repetitive pattern, and that pattern is created by an internal pattern of repeating shapes. The edge and the internal repeating pattern are entirely interdependent and create the whole reason for the design of the rug.

I think that if you were to scale up this rug idea, it would make a fabulous hall runner, or stair carpet. Measure your stairs and make the individual motif elements fit into the treads and rises. Then use stair rods or poles to hold your rug in place.

This design is constructed using a leaf and a circle pattern, but you could change these basic geometric shapes into squares and diamonds, oblongs and ovals, or whatever you like. Draw them out to scale in your sketchbook until you have one which you personally prefer.

Of course, the edges will all have repeating edge shapes that are created by the internal repeating patterns you have designed.

YOU WILL NEED

• *3 lb (1.36 kg) mixed yarns:*
• *4 oz (113 g) of each color—red, blue, yellow, green, purple, turquoise*
• *Brown's tool or equivalent tool*
• *Two pieces of hessian base cloth, measuring 1 x 4 ft (30.4 cm x 1.2 m), plus turnings (see page 120)*
• *Latex*
• *Needle and thread*
• *Scissors*
• *Pattern on page122*

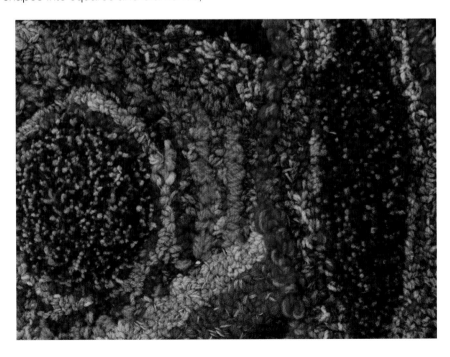

I used different colors for each line in each leaf-shaped motif, as you can see in the close-up photograph right.

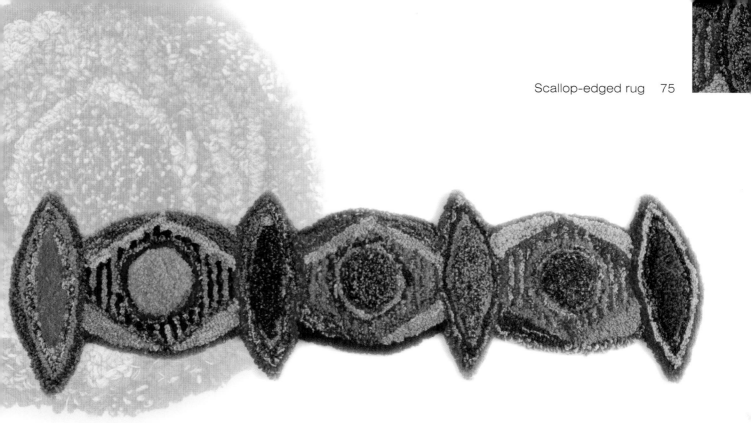

Creating your palette of yarns

Start with 3 lb (1.36 kg) of mixed yarns. I balled up mixtures of four strands of all the yarns I had chosen. I made sure that I had at least two balls of each combination because the areas of cut pile needed more than one ball to make. Therefore the maximum amount of any combination would be 4 oz (113 g). The rug is made by tufting lines that define the pattern, then by infilling those lines. Good, yet unexpected combinations to try are: red, yellow, and blue; red and blue; red and yellow; yellow and red; purple and red; green, red and yellow; turquoise and red; yellow and green. Then also ball up four strands of single colors, or colors where there is one strand of one color and three strands of the other. This makes your palette. This rug is a brilliant way of using up all those odds and ends. Do not be afraid to change colors when you are making up the balls, so if you run out of one shade of blue, then tie in another. This is a traditional carpet-maker and a colorist's technique, and has been used for centuries to be economical.

Nature

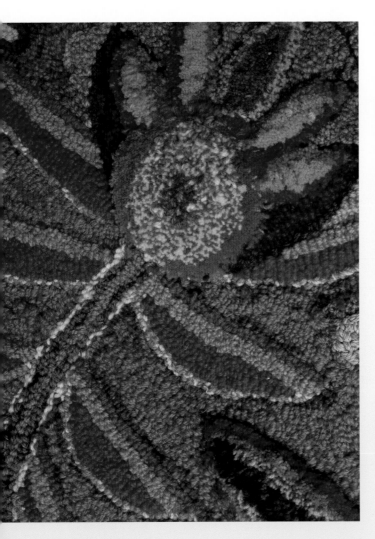

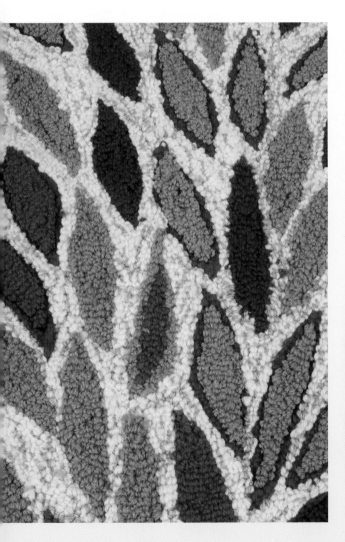

Ecological flocks

Design inspiration can be found in ecological ideas. It can be argued that our systematic interdependence enables us to prevail as a species in the world, but is also the cause of environmental degradation. Environmentalist James Lovelock, originator of the Gaia theory, points out that it is not the earth that will cease to exist, but the viability of human beings. This is because in nature everything is subject to change and everything changes according to its own nature. Metal will rust, plants will biodegrade, and over millennia fossils become oil.

If we want to survive as a species, we need to harness the inherent nature of the materials we use in perpetual cycles of use and reuse. This is difficult when our current systems are totally dependent on market forces. Current thinking looks at how to model new successful and sustainable human systems by studying how flocks, shoals, herds, and other groups of animals change behavior when threatened, and work together in order to survive and flourish.

Consider a shoal of fish: while they always relate to each other, each fish is entirely separate and independent, yet able to make a split-second response to any fish and movement around it. Every fish has the capacity to be the first to respond to danger—a shark, for example— and will trigger an almost instantaneous reaction, like a shimmer throughout the shoal, from one fish to the next and so on, so that they all act as one to move away from the danger.

In this way, every individual human being has the same power to affect and change the behavior of those around them. Ideas move quickly and take hold almost simultaneously, as collective behavior. To me, the positive element here is that any one of us, if we continue to try and never give up, has the power, as yet not personally realized, to make a change for the better. The key is what that change is, and if it is good, it should be thorough and uncompromising.

I like to play with similar shapes in my sketchbook.

Flock rug

My flock rug is actually made up of leaf, or fish shapes. It is a wonderful exercise to draw lots of leaf shapes, allowing a flow of leaf next to leaf and random pattern building to develop. Every sheet of drawings or rug will have a different flow through it. I like to think that this is an insight into how any group of creatures functions communally as individuals within an accommodating whole.

The use of color here is a design device; the shapes are all the same but I love to play with the extremes of blue, namely turquoise and a cobalt blue which is beginning to turn into lilac. The background of the rug is a mixture of cream and pale blue because I didn't want the white to dominate, and also for practical reasons; when this rug is used on the floor, stains aren't going to show as much.

Red, white and blue are fantastically evocative colors to work with. Matisse and Braque and Picasso knew this. Think of the beautiful blue cutouts of birds that these artists created.

Tonally, the red acts in the same way as a black line because it is quite dark, but red is also the most vibrant color to use against other colors to set them off. Actresses on stage use this device to make their eyes look bright; they place a small spot of red in the corner. Also using a tiny amount of red in any painting is often subconsciously picked up by the eye and therefore a painting looks much more vibrant because of it.

The use of the red and the use of the different blues allows the eye to focus on different groups within the overall pattern and flit from one group to another. For example, if you look at the rug, first focus on all the red edges, then focus on all the darkest blue, and then focus on all the turquoise. There's a lovely sense of movement in the design. To develop your own designs, use other shapes in flocks.

YOU WILL NEED

- 9^1/$_2$ lb (4.3 g) mixed yarns:
- 5^1/$_2$ lb (2.5 g) white or cream
- 2 lb (907 g) turquoise
- 1^1/$_2$ lb (680 g) blue
- 8 oz (225 g) red
- Brown's tool or equivalent tool
- Two pieces of hessian base cloth, measuring 6 x 3 ft (1.8m x 90 cm), plus turnings (see page 120)
- Latex
- Needle and thread
- Scissors
- Pattern on page 123

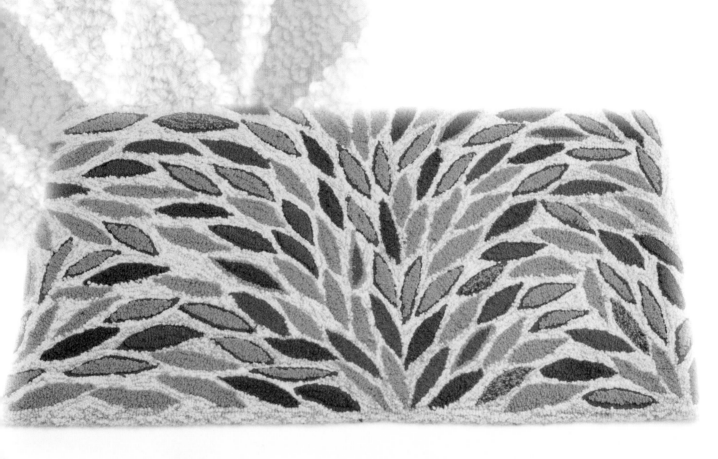

Flowers

Flowers are transcendental; they are miracles, like slow fireworks, with color, form, structure, pattern, and inspiration. They have a sense of life and animation and also allude to parallel interpretations. A pencil drawing of a colored flower will bring pathways of decorative source material that are unimaginable.

I love to draw and paint flowers in a traditional way, where I set up a still life and conduct an observational exercise. In some cases, the attempt at accuracy is constantly undermined. I can go off into a physical reverie, seduced by the medium—watercolor on slightly damp paper is an exquisite battle between control and sensuality— or I can try to keep control, and then use the resulting painting as primary reference for further investigations.

Flowers have been an abiding inspiration in most decorative art throughout the centuries. Intellectual ideas can be used to mediate our creative interpretations, perhaps analytical drawing disciplines, or other systems or methods. We can apply an idea and follow it like a game in order to develop diversity in our visual language. For example, we can use only straight lines to define an otherwise curved source; we can simplify, or stretch, or employ symmetry. Stylization, asymmetry, blocks of color, formal repeats, changing color combinations, increasing or decreasing scale, and using grids all add visual diversity.

In many ways, the colors of flowers simply take over. I cannot think of anywhere else in nature where the diversity of color is so profligate, and we only see a small part of what is visible to us. There are infrared lines and ultraviolet patterns on petals that can only be seen by insects.

These are sketchbook pages of watercolors and pencil drawings of flowers. In the painting I am enjoying the sensuality of the paint, water, and brush. In the pencil sketch, I am analyzing as I draw with a view to formal stylization. Some patterns can be drawn from an observational process, but really bear very little reference to the original source. The drawings are the proverbial "first steps" that we need to take if we are to walk around the world, or in this case make exciting patterns, rugs, textiles, and paintings.

Fleurs des fantasies rug

My flower rugs are a way of using as much color as possible in imaginary forms. I am carrying on a tradition of making fantasy, floral motifs that dates back to pre-Islamic times within the Persian Empire. The Sassanid empire (224–652) claims the *boteh*, which is an early form of the paisley motif, based on a cypress or mango tree, or an asymmetric flower. The paisley shape is fantastic to work with: I fill its shape with other flowers or patterns, I curl lines and spirals inside it and outside it. I join it to imagined stems, mirror it, partner it, and repeat it. It is so fantastic because of its asymmetry, which is eternally suggestive and flirtatious.

The flowering tree of wish fulfilment in the garden of Eden is the core theme in oriental carpets. The stylization of forms, which probably occurred because of the actual techniques needed to create tufts in a grid form, are even more elaborate, extravagant, and fluid in exquisite Indian chintz palampores. As more people wanted these beautiful patterns and textiles around them, print manufacturers in Marseilles, France, went on to mass-produce calico fabrics for the European market.

In Europe, early fantasy floral wallpapers imitated tapestries. The Victoria and Albert Museum in London is full of wonderful and inspirational examples of Spitalfields' silks, William Morris' curling plant forms, Rococo extravagancies, damask, Indian chintz, and embroideries. Elizabethan embroideries are also exquisitely stylized, and yet another source of inspiration. Chinoiserie was the decorative influence of stylization from China from the seventeenth century onward, manifest in ceramics, lacquerwork, and painting.

In the early seventeenth century, Mughal emperor Shah Jehan asked for the naturalist flower paintings by the artist Mansur to be developed into decorative motifs.

It is almost impossible to ignore fantasy flowers. It is marvelous to sit for a few hours and let your imagination go wild with shapes, forms and colors. I shoot the flowers into the plane of the rug, suggesting that they are only one small selection of an eternal dance of *fleurs de fantasie* shooting in with *joie de vivre*, and bursting into life like fireworks.

YOU WILL NEED

- *7 lb (3 kg) yarn (mixed blues)*
- *4–6 oz (113–170 g) of each color*
- *Brown's tool or equivalent tool*
- *Two pieces of hessian base cloth, measuring 2 x 5 ft (60 cm x 1.5 m), plus turnings (see page 120)*
- *Latex*
- *Needle and thread*
- *Scissors*
- *Pattern on page 123*

Creating your palette of yarns

Use mixed blues for the background. Graduate these from the turquoise to lavender blue range of the spectrum by mixing four strands together, and changing the colors by breaking one strand and adding a slightly different blue at intervals. Maybe make four changes throughout one hand-sized ball of yarn. This graduates the background effectively. All the other yarns in the rug are left-over ends. You need about 4–6 oz (113–170 g) of each color. Mix these together in the same way as the mixing of balls of yarn on the scallop-edged rug on page 74. Look at the photographs of the rug and use the pattern above to transfer the design to your backing cloth.

In this series of fleurs de fantasies rugs, I packed the color densely, and did a lot of intricate cut pile. I had collected lots of remnants from industrial dye houses until I had enough to go to town with bright colors. I used the color to maximize contrast and make the colors sing with a sense of joy. I like the idea that I make something, a conversation where I express intense happiness, then send it off into the world where it will meet with, carry that message to, and talk to other people for years to come.

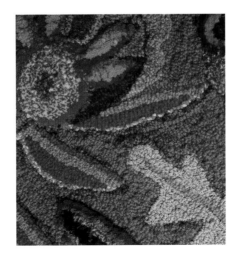

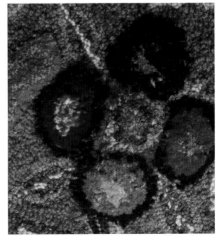

Children's workshop

This workshop can be a party, a craft club activity, a project for charity, a school project, a workshop at a fair or festival, something to do for a group of friends on a rainy day or weekend, or youth club fun—in fact, it's a brilliant thing to offer to any group of kids who like to make things, or didn't even know that they liked to make things!

Checklist
- Scissors
- Brown's hand-tufting tools
- Select balls of yarns and rag strips (aesthetically harmonious so that the final rug looks as good as possible)
- Markers for drawing designs onto the fabric
- Squares of backing fabric about 18 in (45 cm) square (hessian or professional backing cloth)
- Paper and pencils
- Table and chairs for everyone
- Newspapers or cloth to protect the table

Tips
- The tools are quite sharp so protect the table, or ask the kids to work on mats that are large enough for their work.
- The children should not get injured, but it's a good

idea to have antiseptic cream and Band-Aids on hand.
• Don't let the kids get tired, keep them engaged and
concentrating, and make sure they all have picked up
the technique.
• Let them have a break to eat, drink, and talk about
what they are doing.
• Ask some adults to help (and join in).
• A good lighting source is important.

Instructions for teaching the workshop

First lay the yarn out in the center of the table, and put
some backing cloth, scissors, paper, pencil, and a
marker at each place. Ask the kids to do a few quick
paper drawings of designs of flowers. You may want
to provide inspirational source materials—books
or finished rugs—or just let them use their own
imagination: either way is fine. They might want to copy
what you show them. This is fine if your objective is to
have more control over the outcome, but it can set up
a stress level where they are not sure if they are doing
something well enough. I prefer to let them use their
own imagination, and then they are not trying to tick
a box, or reach some invisible level of achievement.
Creativity should flow from inside rather be pulled out.
Some children have low levels of confidence; this is
an opportunity to let them try to actually do something
for themselves. Help and encouragement might be
just what a child needs. Although, beware of piling on
too much praise, at least until you see that they have
accomplished something for themselves. Try also to
keep praise evenly spread, but expressed differently to
each child in the group, so that each one feels special.

Ask the children to draw their flower design (about
6–9 in/15–19 cm in diameter) onto the backing cloth.
Show them an example, leaving a border around the

flower. It should be possible to complete a tufted flower in a three-hour workshop. Carla, one of the children in our workshop, was so enthusiastic and capable that she made two flowers!

Give a demonstration of the tool. Ask them to look at the tool, and tell them what each part is for. Then ask them to squeeze the two handles together to release the jaws of the tool, and explain that this catches the yarn to pull it through. The point goes through the fabric beyond the door of the latch. Next, ask them to press the handles together and carefully place the yarn between the jaws. Before they let go the handles, tell them to be careful not to get their fingers caught between the jaws.

Demonstrate the process and explain about how many threads of backing fabric go through. The tufting is

conducted at 90-degree angles to the lines that they have drawn. Give the children enough information so that they can begin to have a go themselves.

I showed the children the process, and then went around the group one by one, working from behind with both of my hands in front of each child. Using my own tool, I asked them to copy what I was doing with their tool. If necessary, I gently helped each child by holding their hands in the required positions through each action. Then I let them do it themselves, being encouraging, informative, and focused, waiting until I felt they had the basic understanding before moving on to help the next child. I answered questions from other children, but stayed with each child in turn to fairly share my time and attention.

I went around the group once more, checking and offering remedial help. When most of the children had mastered the basic skills, I concentrated on helping those children who were struggling a bit. However, it is important to leave them to work it out for themselves to a certain extent because, unlike intellectual learning, this is a skill where the hands learn, and the mind works in a different way. If I had been perpetually hovering, the child would not have been able to let his or her hands, eyes, and brain engage in the skill with a "physical understanding." Understanding by doing is different from understanding by thinking.

For some, it can be easy to lose heart if the other kids seem to be making their flowers quickly. I asked any children who looked disheartened if they would let me do a few stitches for them to show them what it should look like. This helped because they could catch up with the others, and what I had done was a visible reward for the effort they had already put in. They also had an opportunity to watch my hands while applying their newly found "physical understanding."

Let the kids have a break. Do a show-and tell-during the

break, or let them take a complete rest if need be.

You can introduce ideas about recycling while the workshop is in progress, but do it by asking the kids to tell you what they know, and just manage the discussion.

Finishing the rug

Ask the kids to write their names on their work, and make a note for future reference. You may have to finish some of the pieces yourself. Trim and turn in the edges of the flowers. Arrange them on a fresh piece of backing cloth, and sew the flowers down. Tuft and embellish the background as you wish. I decided that a medium blue worked well with all the colors in the flowers. I added a few star shapes to break up the larger areas around the flowers. You might decide to tuft stem and leaf shapes or other flowers or motifs, arrange as a bouquet, make each flower into the petal of one big flower, or use the flowers as a border.

You can latex the back of the rug, and use it as a wall hanging or a rug!

I finished some of the children's work. These photographs show how far two of the children got with their projects during the four-hour party. They learned how to do it, had cake and lunch, chatted, and spent two hours tufting.

See how the yarn and the rag are used together and also the different pile heights. We sometimes cut the pile and sometimes leave it looped.

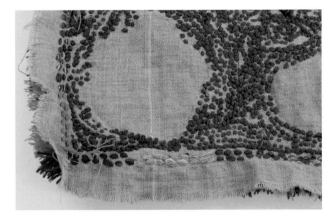

Sew the children's flowers onto the backing cloth and tuft around them. This is what the back looks like.

Animal profiles

Animal profiles are evocative and beautiful images and lend themselves really well to making a simple and stunning rug. In terms of style, I think they cross a lot of boundaries. The white horse (see page 12) can hold its own in chic, minimalist interiors in London and New York, as well as in bohemian apartments in Paris, a horse ranch in Argentina, and the bedroom of a horse-loving teenager or young child. Getting a good silhouette is the key, followed by making an appropriate background. My rug of a hare's shadow (see page 94–5) is made from soft alpaca that is naturally black, so no dyes have been used. It's environmentally very sound because the animals live in the UK, and the yarn is made by John Arbon Textiles, using a renovated water mill. The background is tufted to look like the striped and textured soil of a freshly plowed field.

You could make the silhouette of a bird and set it against the sky; a stag against a forest or sky; a fish against swirling patterns of water; a cat curled in a basket, or a dog running along the brow of a hill. In a series of animal silhouette preparatory designs, I used vintage fabrics, and only blocked out part of the original pattern to create a visual harmony of color and pattern. Translating another art form, such as painting or collage, into rug making is a great way of extending your aesthetic versatility further than your preconceptions. You also end up with paintings *and* a rug!

One of the reasons for using a silhouette is that you don't have the problem of translating the intricacies of a detailed drawing into a medium that is quite chunky. Also, by positioning the animal profile as if it is "floating," and by making it into a decorative motif, it is simpler to assimilate into an interior in design terms—it's often easier to place the rug on the floor, when it does not have to be seen from just one point of view. To create a rug that can be viewed from all directions, consider various juxtapositions of more animal silhouettes. I favor the use of two elements as a design foil.

Among the great exponents of simple animal silhouettes are George Braques, Pablo Picasso, Jean Cocteau, and the decorative genius Jean Dunand. I love the sculpture of British artist Nicola Hicks too. Stylized animals can also be found in Coptic tapestries, medieval bestiaries, books of hours, and medieval tapestries. In addition, photographic stills from nature, television programs, and analytical photography, such as the movement studies of Eadweard Muybridge, are great sources for good silhouettes. You can, of course, change or adapt these, using artistic license. A useful trick is to look at the reflections of your drawings in the mirror to make sure that the images look well balanced. It is also a way of catching ourselves unawares, of seeing any glaring mistakes. I always used to do this when doing life drawings or portraits.

Bird brooch by Annette O'Sullivan, Hare brooch by Annie Sherburne and Mark Gladwell, C19th Dragon saucer.

Hare rug

I like to make a hare rug for my shop every February. The winter is usually cold, and dragging on, but the evenings are getting lighter, and when I am woken at 6.30 a.m. by the alarm it isn't dark outside anymore. It's a slow crawl into spring. But the fields are plowed, there's frost on the furrows, and shadows delineate the topography of the land. Sometimes there are flecks of chalk, and later in spring a faint bloom of tiny green shoots. But now, the ground is linear like corduroy, and now is the time to spot the long-footed, long-eared shadow of a hare, harbinger of spring, waiting to leap in madness.

I make my hare rugs with eco yarns. The hare is made from the crudest and the most luxurious of yarns—hand-spun wild hemp and alpaca from UK herds, spun in Devon using a renovated waterwheel. Smooth and soft, and harsh, too, both feelings at the same touch.

The undulations are double lines of low loop pile and high cut pile mixes of discarded carpet yarn. I do the tuft test (see page 45) to help me choose two combinations of colors and textures that go well together, and then draw parallel lines on the rug backing. This is a surprisingly simple, yet effective design to make. I like the edges to "meander," looking a bit like the soft and spreading edges of handmade paper. I positioned the hare off-center, as if he were about to leap off the edge of the rug, just like the ethereal appearances of the creature itself.

YOU WILL NEED

- *8 lb (3.6 kg) mixed brown yarn (for the field)*
- *4 lb (1.8 kg) mixed beige yarn (for the field)*
- *8 oz (225 g) black alpaca and hand-spun wild hemp (for the hare)*
- *Brown's tool or equivalent tool*
- *Two pieces of hessian base cloth, measuring 6 x 3 1/2 ft (1.8m x 1 m), plus turnings (see page 120)*
- *Latex*
- *Needle and thread*
- *Scissors*
- *Pattern on page 124*

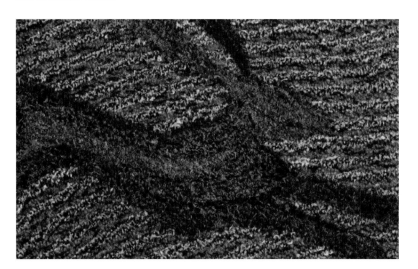

The texture of the yarns as well as the color make the hare silhouette. When you touch the soft alpaca and the harsh hemp, you feel the contrast too.

Creating your palette of yarns

The hare is made from black alpaca and hand-spun wild hemp that was dyed with black natural dyes (8 oz/225 g in total). The field is comprised of double stripes of two different sets of mixed yarns. Do a test with what you have to find a good combination of a mix of four single yarns that go with another mix of four single yarns. You need twice as much of one (8 lb/3.6 kg) than the other (4 lb/1.8 kg) because this will be a high pile that you will cut.

Shells and the seashore

Shells, like flowers, are amazingly beautiful and inspiring. The structures are so curious, suggesting geometry and symmetry, but never quite being that perfect. They are, however, perfect in their own way, belying that graphic obsession that goes with architecture or science, or the achievements of straight lines and mathematical measurements. Natural, integral, übercool, calcified extrusions of crustacea, eroded by the sea, satisfyingly solid, robust, full of secret places, and having the subtle dynamic symmetry that is also present in the paisley pattern. If you look at shells, they give a sense of home, yet at the same time, a feeling of potential movement. Little caravans of perfect forms.

I love to draw shells. Their shapes are abundantly open to interpretation, and also marvelously challenging to try to capture uniquely and with verisimilitude.

Draw them from all angles, and you have a decorative dictionary of forms and shapes that will be sympathetic to arrangements and authentic pattern designs.

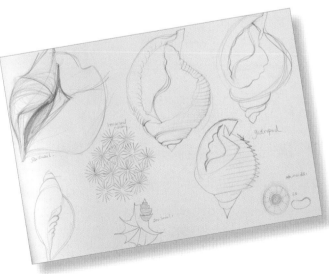

I found these lovely copperplate illustrations at Spitalfields market. The forms are so amazing—they look like space-age citadels to me!

I love drawing the forms of shells, they are so inspiring, and my hand wants to dance with a good sharpened soft lead pencil, enjoying the new shapes that my subjects suggest. I stylize as I draw—I am not trying to make my drawing look like a photograph, I want to play with forms and patterns.

Shell-shaped bag

The inspiration for this bag came from making pompoms. I thought, why not make flat velvet fabric by using the technique of wrapping threads around a cardboard form, and then cutting to make a velvety pile?

I cut strips of cardboard, from approximately 1/4 in (3/4 cm) wide to 1/2 in (1cm) wide. I graduated the width of these strips of cardboard to make what I hoped would be an undulating velvet surface. It turns out that the graduated effect is negligible, and I would not advise that you go to these lengths. I designed a fan-shaped shell for this new technique. The stripes emulate the ribs of a scallop shell.

The secret to making the technique work is to sew a few lines next to each other before cutting the pile but leave the edges of each section looped, and around their cardboard cores. This holds the tufting that you have made in place.

YOU WILL NEED

- *Hessian backing cloth, at least 6 ins (15 cm) larger all around than the pattern.*
- *A few large-eyed sewing needles*
- *Cardboard*
- *Embroidery threads: a mixture of cottons, silks, rayon, and artificial s*
- *Suitable fabric for back and lining*
- *Scissors*

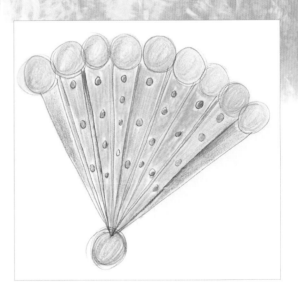

Left: A close-up of the velvet surface. I like to wear the velvet bag as if it's a piece of jewelry.

Above: This color work looks complicated but it is systematic. When you understand what simple rules underpin the pattern it is easier to do than it seems! This is an interplay between hot and cool colors.

Making the bag

It takes time, but this is a sweet project because you are making a very special and fine handmade velvet.

In my design, there are stripes that fan out. At their apex, there is little room for all the colors in the fan, so I make sure that the defining lines meet there (the ribs, as it were), and then fill in the other lines farther up from the apex of the design. This looks like lots of elongated V-shapes.

Before you begin

Draw the basic fan and spokes. Thread a fat-eyed needle with a couple of doubled strands of embroidery thread, old sewing thread, or fine yarn. Place a cardboard strip along a line.

2 Keep repeating step 1 until you have covered the whole cardboard strip. If you look on the other side, you should be pleased with a neat line of little stitches—not perfectly aligned like a sewing machine, but slightly and sweetly different one to the next in a nonetheless orderly fashion.

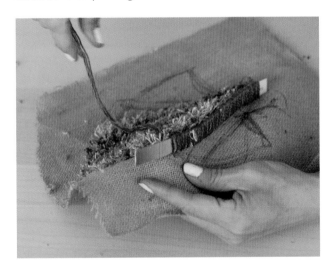

1 Sew the thread around the cardboard strip, and through the fabric base fabric: Catch only one or two hessian warp threads and bring the threaded needle back up on the other side of the cardboard strip. Leave the end loose, but just hold it gently—you don't need a knot because you are making a fabric of lots of cut ends. Keep the cardboard strip aligned with your drawn line.

3 Working along the top of the cardboard strip, cut the threads, remove the cardboard strip and start the next row.

I made pompoms (see page 54) to edge the bag, and bought some old necklaces from a vintage stall to make a tassel and the strap.

I see this bag as practical jewelry—a sort of Amazonian necklace. You can put your keys and some money in it, wear it across a plain dress, and dance the night away!

4 Cut the pile. To finish, cut a piece of complimentary fabric (I used printed felt) and hand sew the pre-turned edges together with a simple Cretan or fine blanket stitch.

Our world

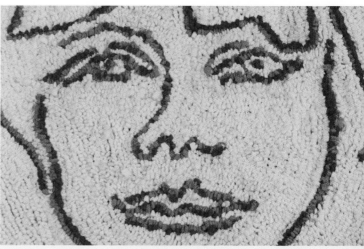

People

People, faces, and interpretations of human beings are often used as design motifs. From simple stick figures holding hands on hand-knitted sweaters, to artist Rob Ryan's fabulous paper cutouts. Mermaids, fantastical fairies, angels, cupids, and cartoon characters—all these are good inspirational sources for rugs.

Until now, my personal preference when using any sort of human form has been to use a very stylized face. I say until now, because you will see quite a naturalistic approach to the human form in the rug that I have designed and made for this book (pages 106–7).

In the inspiration section, I have picked pieces from work by my family and friends. The child's drawing is by my eldest son, Josiah. He made this drawing of his second girlfriend, Tegan. In development terms, this illustrates a diagrammatic approach to the way a child notates what they see in the world. The first drawing is a round face with eyes and lips. Here there is notating and counting occurring, a smiling face, body, legs, arms, and fingers! We made jewelry from the drawings that both kids did, and examples of all Joe's work were bought by Rutgers University to illustrate stages of cognitive awareness in childrens' drawings.

Above: Drawing by Josiah Sherburne-Gladwell, aged 3.

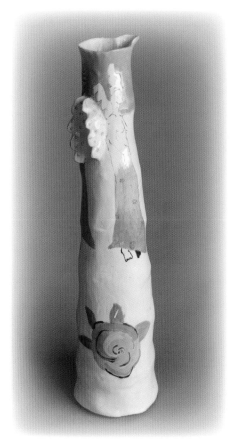

Left: Angel vase by Edla. Right: Handbag and Mirror are my designs. Coffee bowl by Mike Levy and Christopher Corr. Moon by Candlelight by Julie Arkell. Plate by Sylph Bear.

Face rug

I often take my sketchbook with me when I go on vacation. I enjoyed drawing my children and I have used two of these drawings as the source material for this rug. You could use a good photograph of your subject's face if you are not confident in your drawing skills.

Put the tracing paper onto your drawing or photograph. Trace the edge of the face, the edge of the hair, the edges of the lips, the line between the lips, the neckline, and a bit of shoulder if you would like to add that to your composition. The most important part to capture the character will be the eyes. Pay close attention to drawing the upper lid line and then the lower lid line in relation to the shape of the pupil. Be discerning and critical and try to see only the actual shapes that are there, not what you think the shapes should be! The character is also expressed in the line of the brow. Bring that line down to the top of the line of the nose, and make one line to define the profile of the nose. Then choose to make one confident line to define the outside shape of the bottom of the nose, from the point where it folds to meet the cheek, and then around to define the two dips of the nostrils. I find noses difficult to draw because without shadows to define their form there are no obvious "edges" to them. Don't worry! Be confident, be simple, and if you need encouragement, look at masters of simplicity like Matisse, Picasso, or Cocteau!

From now on the process is simple. Make a grid over your tracing, and enlarge this onto the backing cloth to the size you want your rug to be.

I am so pleased with this piece. I will be putting it onto my wall rather than onto the floor!

I love this piece—I'm going to put it on the wall as I don't want to walk on my childrens' faces.

YOU WILL NEED

- *10 lb (4.5 kg) old sheets ripped into strips (for the background)*
- *2 lb (907 g) old red fabric ripped into strips (for the face)*
- *1 lb (453 g) red yarn (for definition)*
- *Brown's tool or equivalent tool*
- *Two pieces of hessian base cloth, measuring 6 x 3 1/2 ft (1.8 x 01 m), plus turnings (see page 120)*
- *Latex*
- *Needle and thread*
- *Scissors*
- *Your photograph or drawing, scaled up (see pages 22-3)*

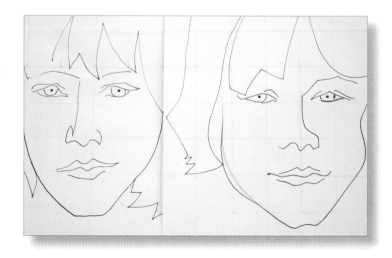

Objects

The graffiti around where I live in London 's East End, along with imaginary creatures that my kids have collected over the years, are just so joyful that I decided to invent my own graffiti letters and my own creatures and characters.

You can do the same, perhaps making drawings of your children's favorite cuddly toys, but you can also take any source material that you like and transform it into a rug design—your ideas are only limited by your imagination. The images of creatures here are quite simple to draw. Sometimes people are intimidated by the word "design" or the idea of being a "designer," but we didn't worry about that when we were kids and were given pieces of paper and paints and crayons, so why worry about it now? Most people are going to be making rugs as part of recreation, enjoyment, not work, and certainly not to be judged by. Of course, we all want to feel proud of what we have done, but there is nothing to stop us quietly enjoying making something anyway. We don't have to show it, but people love to see something original. I know I do. I love seeing other's work. People come into my shop and show me what they have made using the eco knitting yarns I used to sell there. My interns and students show me their work. It's like sharing ideas in conversation, and everyone's ideas are different and fascinating to someone else. The very act of making something *is* in itself inspirational.

So, just look around you. What do you like? What do you think is funny? What is personal or special to you? Do a line drawing of it, and try a small rug. Why not!

Baby rug

Making special textiles to welcome a new baby is a wonderful tradition. It is another opportunity for a group to create a rite of passage. Life is full of narratives. I love meeting new people, and I love getting to know older friends and relations, and finding time and space to be together and hear their stories. When we get together to mark a special occasion, and when we sit down to make something together, we are doing something very powerful. In making a rug for a baby, we are making memories for ourselves and we are making a space in our hearts into which we can welcome the new addition to the family. The rug will hold memories of the journey we took together while waiting for the baby to arrive. For the child, the rug will hold memories of love from their family forever. It is so important.

This project can be good for individuals to make, too, and does not have to be a group effort. I remember the last month of my pregnancy, when keeping occupied was particularly important. I wasn't too well; I had pre-eclampsia, which is a life-threatening condition. Making things helped me to keep calm.

YOU WILL NEED

- *1lb (453 g) white (for the background)*
- *2 oz (56 g) of each color*
- *8 oz (225 g) turquoise*
- *Brown's tool or equivalent tool*
- *Two pieces of hessian base cloth, measuring 18 x 12 in (45 x 30 cm), plus turnings (see page 120)*
- *Latex*
- *Needle and thread*
- *Scissors*
- *Pattern on page 124*

With this particular project, there is also an opportunity to design a rug that is bit kitsch. A witty and contemporary influence can be found in the craze for creating and collecting Toon-like animals, or manga-influenced, big-eyed characters. Even more cutting-edge is the new era of spray-painted graffiti creatures, gleaming with gaudy and ironic innocence. There are also Amos toys, anime plastic dolls, comic books like Vortigern's Machine, Silas figures, and Tokyoplastic figures, all of which are collectible, and have influenced the slightly offbeat, ironic, soft toys, with button eyes or slight mutations, which have been appearing for the last few years. I am not advocating scaring babies, but hoping to stimulate the design process, and "radical cute" would make really good adult interior design pieces.

Lettering

When we look at letters on the page, their primary purposes are to communicate ideas, which are brought to life by using words. The shapes and marks of those words and letters are also visually fascinating. They can be comforting, too, because they are shapes we recognize, and like the sound of drums that speak to our heartbeats, they are visually, as well as intellectually, fundamental.

The history of decorated lettering goes back to illuminated manuscripts, and to the evolution of writing across history, where scripts often developed from simplified pictorial representations of the natural world. As designers we can use these ideas as well, as visual inspiration to stimulate what we do and make.

If we strip away the intellectual equivalent and concentrate on the shapes, we can use letters as roots for creative shape-making. We can do what the brilliant street artists do, namely, create our own letters, alphabets, and signifiers of meaning. Our own names are uniquely ours, so why not change the shapes of the way our names are written? We all do this when we experiment with writing our signature! The letters can be unique to us, without losing the power to communicate their commonly

Above and opposite: graffiti from East London that inspired the alphabet I sketched (right).

understood meaning. This is another chance to celebrate differences between all of us, to create our own identities, and to evolve visual language. On the street, people write their names as tags. They notate their journey, make their mark, show bravery, foolhardiness, and wit, albeit illegally!

Our new alphabets and scripts can also be used to spell out meaning beyond the aesthetic. This is the art of font designers, typesetters, stone and wood carvers, and poets. We can be visual rappers.

I love to make shapes, so using the alphabet was a great structure to begin an exploration of lettering. I think I could have filled many sketchbooks while playing and exploring the possibilities. Try to make a spiky alphabet, or one that incorporates arrows, or one that wobbles, or whirls. Make shadows behind your letters, make them 3-D, and then there are the endless possibilities for pattern and color in every letter! Graduate the color, add stripes, make cartoon characters! Do lots—that's what a sketchbook is for!

Words and letters rug

I am lucky to live in the heart of London, England. I live in Shoreditch, which is full of clubs, bars, and artists and designers. It is gritty as well as culturally vibrant, and has some of the most diverse and extensive radical graffiti and street art of any city on the planet. If you know your street art—you may even be a graffiti tourist—you will find that there is a lot to see in the area (see box below).

One artist, known as Eine, has decorated the metal shutters of shops all around London with enlarged letters of the alphabet in his own recognizable font.

My letter rug is just one letter. You can download an elaborate font from the internet or design your own, then scale it up and make a contemporary and iconic statement inspired by the radical street art of London. Make square letters and fit them together to make words. The possibilities for creativity in rug making are limitless.

> ## YOU WILL NEED
> - *2 lb (907 g) mixed yarn for the background*
> - *2 lb (907 g) mixed yarn for the letter*
> - *Brown's tool or equivalent tool*
> - *Two pieces of hessian base cloth, measuring 5 x 5 ft (1.5 x 1.5 m), plus turnings (see page 120)*
> - *Latex*
> - *Scissors, needle and thread*
> - *Pattern on page 125*

East London street art

If you are ever in East London, look out for the tiny figurines usually found in a model maker's store. These tiny people have been arranged here and there to make vignettes of life, looking into the edges of puddles, sitting on the grill of an underground train's heating radiator, or contemplating the huge drop from a stucco molding outside a pub. There are amazing Bombay Babylon bejeweled gods and goddesses, reliefs on derelict buildings along Brick Lane, and crocheted legwarmers on lampposts. There are poly bag weavings on wire fences, and a series of giant rodents spray-painted on the sides of buildings that have become landmarks.

Creating your palette of yarns

The background accounts for the larger
quantities of yarn in this rug, and is mixed by
using stripes as pattern. This means that by
clever mixing of smallish quantities of colors
that you have already you can make up
enough yarn to create the backgrounds and
the letter effectively. Allow 2 lb (907 g) for the
background, and 2 lb (907 g) for the letter.

Bachelorette party rug

I found a fantastic bar in Shoreditch, London, called the Book Club for the bachelorette party rugmaking session. Downstairs, I set up tables. There was music, a constant flow of cocktails, and the potential to have a DJ, but everyone was keen to catch up with news, remember the bride's childhood and her single life, and, of course, make the rug that would be an amalgam of everyone's memories.

Every guest had been asked to bring a garment that reminded her of the bride. Some brought things that reminded them of their own lives! Great conversations and memories poured out. I set up the table with yarns, and laid out gray backing cloth, a heart template, black markers, and rugmaking tools.

Above, from left to right: The bride's sister reminds the party about the origin of the garment she has brought to use for her part of the heart rug. The bride's mother works out how to cut her fabric into strips to tuft with. Grandma wore the cutest ears, and while she worked she remembered delightful stories from the bride's childhood. The bride cut up a great pair of the groom's pants which she had appropriated from his drawers that very morning.

Friends, aunts, and neighbors all learned quickly how to make the little heart rugs. Conversation, cocktails, and laughter flowed.

The table was covered so that the markers did not mark through the cloth. People were asked to draw around the heart template and then I showed everyone how to tuft.

I made an example of a finished heart to show everyone. The hearts are to be sewn together after with spaces in between, or, in effect, "holes" in the final rug. This is a great contemporary twist on rugmaking because the floor that the rug is placed on shows through and creates a unity to the otherwise often very different pieces that people make. I would advise that in order to maintain a harmony in terms of color that the bride ask people to bring garments and items to include in their tufting that are, as far as possible, within a particular color range. It may be that the chosen item is so emotionally charged that the guest wants to use it even if it is in a different color range, and since this rug is marking a rite of passage within people's lives, it should be included. My solution to this was to have a bright, full-spectrum palette, and make a "jolly" rug. I think that because it is colorful, this rug would eventually look lovely in a child's bedroom.

There were lovely comments during the party. Here are a few memories of the day:

As the bride, Caroline, started cutting into the pants Doreen sang out "The first cut is the deepest."

Mother-of-the bride Christine decided her

The bachelorette party with their finished hearts at the end of the workshop.

contribution to her daughter's rug would be her wedding dress from the early 1970s. Everyone thought that this was very special. She had bought it in London and when she wore it first Caroline was underneath as a tiny bump! She wore it again to a blessing 18 months ago.

Caroline's sister Corinna suggested using only the skirt of the wedding dress for the rug, and making the top into a new garment!

Family friend Margaret used a fabric that represents Hastings, the seaside town where the bride was brought up.

It would be a good idea to bring a memory book for your bachelorette party, where your guests can write about the fabric that they have contributed.

After the party, I finished the hearts that were unfinished; then I backed them and carefully
arranged them in the most balanced pattern, and then sewed them together.

Patterns and materials

Estimating yarn quantities

Material measurements can only ever be approximate because yarns weigh different amounts and have different thicknesses and lengths. Also, you are encouraged to use yarns from your stash, and to recycle fabrics. This book is a spur to design your own rugs, and so you will be using the designs sometimes as inspiration, and sometimes you will make your own patterns. The patterns shown here and the colors given are simplified as aids to understanding, and are not an exact representation of the rugs in the photographs. Please study the photographs with the patterns if you wish to make more exact copies.

The low-pile, looped rugs require approximately 3/4 lb (340 g) of yarn per square foot (33 x 33 cm) but I would recommend that people always have more yarn than they need, or be prepared to be flexible, and recycle, introduce new materials, and be creative with resources. If you want specific colors, make sure that you acquire enough to begin with or will have access to more if required.

Cut pile rugs will need at least twice as much yarn because there is wastage when the loops are cut and trimmed. If you are making a cut pile, you will need double the weight of yarn you would need for a loop pile, per square foot. Where the pile is very

shaggy, even triple the weight may be needed, for example, when you make the grass for the horse rug on page 12.

Rag rugs need at least 1 lb (453 g) of material per square foot (33 x 33 cm). Cut pile rags often have less wastage because each loop can be cut, but trimming the subsequent work also causes wastage, so I recommend overestimating the material needed.

Estimating background cloth quantities

All rugs require ground cloth of the requisite size, plus extra to turn in at the edges and finish the rug neatly. I recommend at least an extra 4 inches (10 cm) all around. You may also want an extra backing cloth in hessian or another suitable, harder-wearing fabric of the same size to stick onto the back of the finished rug.

Fish rug page 10

2lb (907 g) of mixed yarns and rags

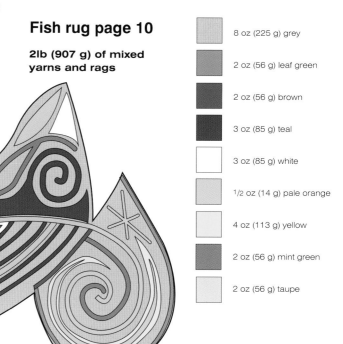

8 oz (225 g) grey

2 oz (56 g) leaf green

2 oz (56 g) brown

3 oz (85 g) teal

3 oz (85 g) white

1/2 oz (14 g) pale orange

4 oz (113 g) yellow

2 oz (56 g) mint green

2 oz (56 g) taupe

Beginner's workshop rug page 41

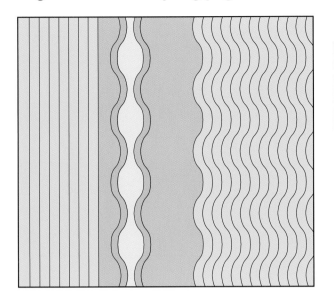

Ogee in mixed yarns

Plain green area

Yellow edging

Circles rug page 60

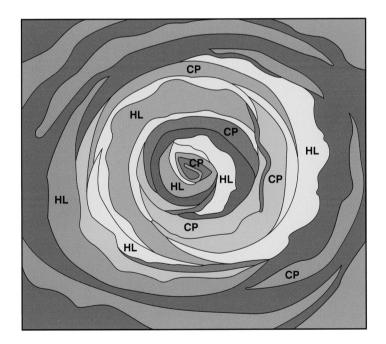

For yarn and rag quantities see project page

HL = High loop

CP = Cut pile

All unmarked areas are low loop

Flower pillow page 54

For yarn and rag quantities see project page

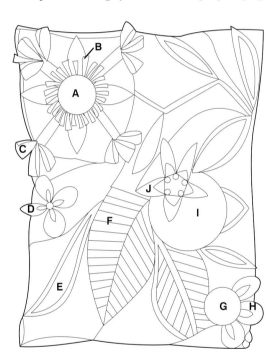

A Pompom
B High cut rag
C Rag high loops
D Fabric metal tufts
E High cut pile rag
F Low cut pile tufts (rag)
G Pompom
H Fabric petal tufts
I Shag high cut pile
J Fabric metal tufts

Scallop-edged rug page 74

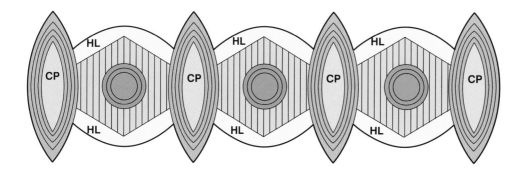

For yarn and rag quantities see project page

HL = High loop

CP = Cut pile

All unmarked areas are low loop

Why the colors work has to do with changing the colors on every stripe. The pattern structure is simple—leaf shapes and circles—but by breaking each shape up with colored stripes a pleasing harmony is achieved. Study the relationships between the colors in the photographs on page 75, then draw out the template and fill each stripe with *your* own colors!

Journey rug page 68

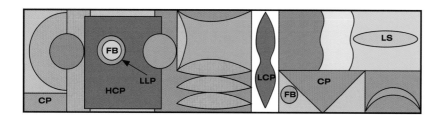

For yarn and rag quantities see project page

CP = Cut pile

HCP = High cut pile

LLP = Low loop pile

FB = Felt ball

LCP = Low cut pile

LS = Leaf shape

Fleurs des fantasies rug page 84

This template is simplified to the major outlines for ease of understanding. Study the inner patterns in the photographs on page 85—or make up your own!

For yarn and rag quantities see project page

CP = Cut pile
All unmarked areas are high loop

Flock rug page 80

Children's workshop rug page 91

Red outline – high loop in the middle only
Other areas are all low loop, including the background

Hare rug page 94

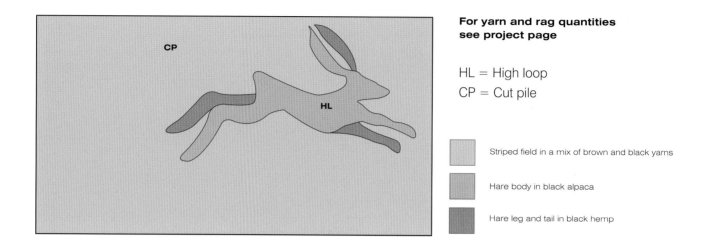

For yarn and rag quantities see project page

HL = High loop
CP = Cut pile

Striped field in a mix of brown and black yarns

Hare body in black alpaca

Hare leg and tail in black hemp

Baby rug page 110

For yarn and rag quantities see project page

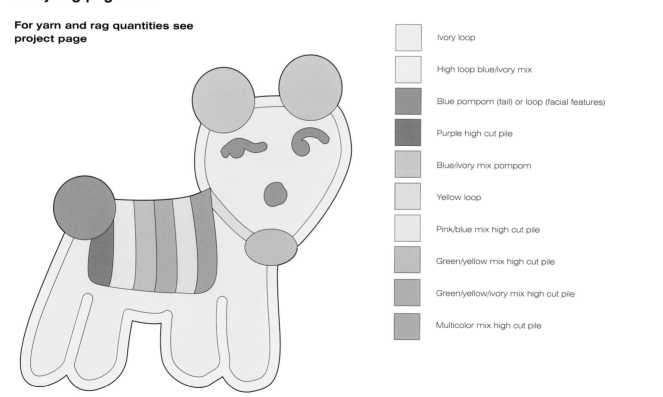

Ivory loop

High loop blue/ivory mix

Blue pompom (tail) or loop (facial features)

Purple high cut pile

Blue/ivory mix pompom

Yellow loop

Pink/blue mix high cut pile

Green/yellow mix high cut pile

Green/yellow/ivory mix high cut pile

Multicolor mix high cut pile

Words and letters rug page 114

For yarn and rag quantities see project page

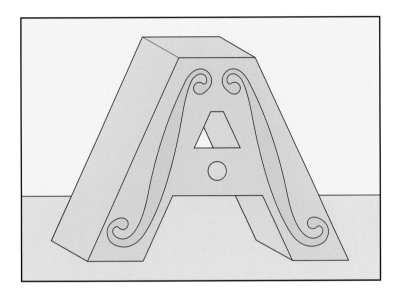

	Alternate 2-color and 4-color vertical stripes
	Alternate 2-color and 4-color horizontal stripes
	Alternate single color vertical stripes
	Dark 2-color mix
	Single color outer stripe and 2-color inner stripe
	Light 2-color mix

Bachelorette party rug page 119

Index

Author's Acknowledgments

Thank you to Judith More for asking me to make this book. Also, darlings Annette O'Sullivan and Liz Cook who have held the biz together, Paul Handley, Simon Harrison, Brendan, Kym Suttle, Monsieur Millwall, Elsie Long, Tim and Ali, Vonney, John Schwiller, Cecile, Chris, Max, Marcus and Frances, Robin G-J, Rachel and Louise at *Prick Your Finger*: all for laughing a lot and parties. Joe and Charlie who kept my heart intact, Markie my dear friend and husband, Kaffe Fassett who opened the doors of color, Ferris Newton who closed the doors of preconception, Jean Muir who showed me why there are few people running on the extra mile, and Boris, Trevor, Sarah Munday, Alan, Rosie and Jenny, and all my beloved friends and family, and to my muse, inspiration and Savior.

Fil Rouge Press would like to thank:

Annie Sherburne for her beautiful rugs, inspiring text and for going the extra mile to produce a wonderful book we are proud to publish.

Maggie Aldred, Jenny Latham, Nina Sharman, Lily More and Allan Titmuss for all their hard work in compiling the project. The folks at Stackpole Books for helping to make the project a reality by taking on the North American edition.

Drink, Shop, Do at 9 Caledonian Road, London N1, The Book Club at Leonard St, London EC2, and Flattime House for their hospitality; Rachel Matthews of Prick Your Finger, 260 Globe Road, London E2.

ANNIE SHERBURNE AT THE OXO TOWER: unit 1.01, first floor riverside, Oxo Tower Wharf, Bargehouse Street, South Bank, London SE1 9PH